# ENQUIRING WITHIN

Also by J. Neville Ward
and published by Epworth Press

*Beyond Tomorrow*
*Five for Sorrow, Ten for Joy*
*The Following Plough*
*Friday Afternoon*
*The Use of Praying*

*J. Neville Ward*

# ENQUIRING WITHIN

EPWORTH PRESS

*To Sarah and Hannah*

*British Library Cataloguing in Publication Data*

Ward, J. Neville (Joseph Neville)
Enquiring within.
1. Christian life
I. Title
248.4

ISBN 0–7162–0452–5

First published 1988
by Epworth Press
Room 195, 1 Central Buildings
Westminster, London SW1H 9NR

Printed in Great Britain by
Richard Clay Ltd, Bungay, Suffolk

# Contents

*Contents*

# *Preface*

I have put together here, loosely arranged, some reflections on the life of faith that have been stimulated mainly by letters but also by questions during retreats and conversations with people attending conferences on spirituality over the last twenty years. Many people have given me the chance of trying to work things out with them or develop at greater length thoughts I had been able only to suggest on some brief occasion. Some of these replies have been combined and some have been extended here, but all of them originated in practical situations of personal need or interest. All such questions may be voiced to some other but are generally found to be addressed within.

66 Mount Road                                    Neville Ward
Canterbury, Kent
1988

# Acknowledgments

The author and publishers are indebted to the following for permission to use copyright material:

Unwin Hyman Ltd for an extract from *W. H. Auden: A Biography* by Humphrey Carpenter;

Burns and Oates Ltd for quotations from *Our Christian Faith* by Karl Rahner and Karl-Heinz Weger;

Faber and Faber Ltd for extracts from *Four Quartets* by T. S. Eliot, *Waiting for Godot* by Samuel Beckett, and *Selected Poems* by John Berryman;

The Tablet Publishing Co. for a poem by Thomas Blackburn;

Sheed and Ward Ltd for an extract from *The Spiritual Letters of Dom John Chapman OSB*.

# TOWARDS THE MIND OF JESUS

# 1 Fantasy, Reality, Maturity

You are certainly not alone in finding Jesus not particularly interesting.

All the way through, Christians seem to have divided into two main spiritual families – those who have felt the seemingly infinite appeal of Jesus, and those who have felt principally the pull of the ultimate *mysterium tremendum et fascinans*.[1] This second group have been amazed at Jesus's curiously intimate relationship with the *mysterium* but have always wanted to talk about it in much less personal, more abstract language than that used by most Jesus-lovers.

Temperamental factors and the way your mind naturally works seem to decide which family is yours. When people discover what their spiritual type is, no one ever seems to move from one to the other, though the discovery itself may involve a move.

I have always felt at home in the second, finding much evangelical talk about Jesus less than beguiling. Every so often, however, someone seems to produce work whose mixed imagery, feeling and belief reach deep within all of us and bring us all marvellously together, whatever our type. I think that Wesley's hymn 'O Thou who camest from above' is one of these marvellously penetrating and uniting things.

Yet certain moments in the New Testament account of

1. A phrase suggested by Rudolf Otto to summarize the mystery, awe and attraction in certain kinds of human experience which lead us to interpret it as experience of the divine.

Jesus seem to me so packed with meaning that he becomes a presence to stir the mind forever, particularly those moments in which he appears to be doing what we also have to do – struggling to understand his experience of life, to find (or regain) himself, and to accept it and genuinely *be* it.

One of them is St Mark's description (1.11,12) of how Jesus, immediately after his baptism, goes straight to the devil and has an awful time with what is called 'temptation'.

Anyone who has what seems to be an experience of God, of being called or chosen or is in some other way given a sense of the glory, of there being in fact something infinitely desirable beyond the grey here and now, will as likely as not soon be led into some kind of wilderness. He'll find himself not knowing quite where he is, certainly feeling alone, and lumbered with this appealing experience that nevertheless has to be sorted out somehow – either dismissed as an emotional episode one mustn't load with too much meaning, or accepted, and itself allowed to suggest what one must do with it.

Lots of people have been there. It's a place where his path crosses ours.

And the account elsewhere of the mental struggle he was then pitched into, the three temptations (Luke 4.1–13), speaks directly to all of us, both when we're at our best and when we're not at our best, particularly when we try to manipulate life and evade the truth.

One of Joseph Conrad's most powerful stories is 'The Shadow-Line'. It concerns among other things the dividing line in the life of everyone who manages to grow up. It's the line between youth and maturity, romance and reality, illusions and the facts of life. I see the temptations story as about Jesus crossing his shadow-line, achieving his manhood by rejecting (and so winning his release from) the fantasy-world of the not-yet-grown-up.

He struggles with three forms of that world's wishful-thinking that hide in our private dream today just as subtly as they did far away and long ago in his – 1. You have only to demand and command and it will be done, 2. if you are compliant you will get what you want, 3. if you fall down you will be picked up.

Those ideas are more or less true in the world of infancy. They are quite false in the adult world, where indeed to succumb to their appeal to the tired spirit amounts to having made a foolish pact with the devil, with anti-life.

Crossing the shadow-line is a matter of realizing this and accepting it with one's whole being, accepting the conditions and limitations of life as lived by most people.

The limitations of religion itself have to be accepted too. Religion is not a matter of favours and compensations that show their pleasant faces in our life because we have got around to believing in God. It is a learning to live fully with life the way it goes, learning to live with the thought of death and the malevolence of things, and learning to live with and interpret all the goodness and hope and sense of an over-all meaning that, like cheerfulness, keep breaking in.

The sense of an over-all meaning, of the almighty importance of life and being alive, comes to each one of us usually in terms of the deal with existence that we have individually had.

For many people it does seem that life has gone in such a pedestrian fashion that they have great difficulty in allowing any experience a possibly transcendent quality and origin. They have made up their minds, or someone has done it for them, that the everyday, its quiet desperation, its occasional beauty, is all there is; and it's now toward evening, and the day is too far spent for them to cope with having their conventional view of things disturbed.

And that really is despair. Somewhere within it is a weeping and angry child.

We grow spiritually as we release ourselves from infantile expectation or infantile hopelessness, and move into faith. This faith is the realization of how things are in this world, for better and worse, and an apprehension (dim at first, never entirely clear) of the over-all meaning Jesus saw in life. When we act in faith, whatever we do, it is not because it will bring us pleasure or divert pain from us, much less because society has programmed us to behave in this way, but because what we are doing emerges from our hold on Jesus's understanding of the truth about life.

# 2 Self-Understanding. Being a Christian

Nowadays I find that Jesus and his teachings have most meaning for me if I interiorize them, interpret them as conveying what it is, and what it could be, to be me right now. There's much more life in them that way than if I see them as related to some vast metaphysical drama, such as humanity's salvation from death's horrible pit through the sacrifice of God's son two thousand years go. Thinking about him like that makes him much less alive, indeed seems just to bury him in doctrine.

The figure in the Gospels is certainly alive. It's not at all surprising that they said he could give people life, or lead them to it or show them how it's done.

He was a free man too, free enough to be honest with his emotions. He was able to complain to his friends for their not being able to watch with him one hour, and he could be generous enough to say at the end of it all, and really gratefully, that they had stood by him in his temptations.

He was able to see life without bitterness from a curious eminence of compassion. One would like to be with him on that height of loving. Yet he was capable of an extraordinary fury – principally, it seems, at rotten religion.

And there's the disturbing decisiveness. He gives you the impression that he knew where he was going, knew this right from the start, although that's hard to believe. At any rate he knew by the time the water of John's baptism had dried on his shoulders.

That can be somewhat formidable. People who see with sharp clarity what they're aiming at can make one shudder.

That's why I'm often drawn to one glimpse of him (Matt.16.13) where he does seem to be letting a bit of uncertainty show through, as though at a quite late hour he was still searching for his identity, and maybe in danger of losing his way.

He turns to his friends for help, for their opinion about the purpose of his being here, what he's supposed to be doing in this shadowy and dangerous time. 'Whom say ye that I am?'

He finds that Peter, for one, has had strong impressions of the eternal and God-like about his strange friend and gropes for the best words he knows to say this – to be greeted immediately by Jesus' eager, happy, grateful response. 'Blessed art thou, Simon Bar-Jona! For flesh and blood have not revealed this to you, but my Father who is in heaven.'

This suggests that the best way to tackle the large questions about Jesus, and, for that matter, ourselves and everybody else, is not by reference to the nexus of flesh and blood, to matters of heredity and social environment, but to the ultimate.

Who and what we are is to be found not by looking at what our ancestry and parents and present circumstances have blessed and doomed us to be, nor at what our not always brilliant coping with experience has made of us, but by means of a religious interpretation of life, referring it all to what Jesus meant by 'my Father in heaven'.

One of the classic Christian answers to this question comes at the beginning of *The Spiritual Exercises of St Ignatius*:

> Man is created to praise, reverence, and serve God our Lord, and by this means to save his soul. All other things on the face of the earth are created for man to help him fulfil the end for which he is created. From this it follows that man is to use these things to the extent that they will help him attain his end. Likewise, he must rid himself of them in so far as they prevent him from attaining it.

That's a theological way of answering the question who and what one is. In terms of spirituality the question sometimes looms much less intellectually, indeed intensely personally. There are periods when the drive of the life-process slackens, and there's a pause and time for thought and a spell of anxiety, and then the question hits hard.

The obvious examples are, at the beginning, with our time at school or college just finished and we are looking for work and what is to be our place in the world; 'in the middle of the journey of our life' when the children have grown up sufficiently not to need their parents so close any more; in retirement, the public role completed, at the close of a poorish day on which not much has happened; and, of course, all through at those times when we surprise and dismay our-selves in some unexpected, unintelligent, perhaps absurd response to experience that we'd like to forget. They are times of great desire to see ourselves correctly and understand.

Among the available clues some are to be found in our regular attitudes. What and who we are within has a lot to do with how we think about our parents, our family, the opposite sex, our work and the time that's not spent at work, trouble (both small irritations and large overwhelmings), whatever makes our heart beat suddenly faster, and (very much vaguer) what we really want from life. If we want to love God, these habitual reactions make up a good deal of what there is in us to love him with.

What we really want from life is the least clear bit of it. We have desires that we are tantalizingly unable to articulate. But these desires figure obscurely in much of what we do.

It seems that our lives are a kind of dream whose latent meaning will become clear only with the help of an interpreter. Though occasionally, in some unusual happiness or excep-tional distress, we know that a moment of truth has come, most of the time we do need someone to help us sort out our life's cloudy symbolism and understand ourselves.

There are many people for whom Christ has been this interpreter, which is a religious way of saying that attempting the Christian way of life has made them feel more real, more expressed, less inhibited, and much more grateful for being in this world. They begin to think that something like this has been what they have been wanting for quite some time.

These interpretations are not arrived at quickly; they take time. There's a famous part of St Augustine's *Confessions* that shows him reflecting on an incident in his life when he was sixteen years of age and stole some pears from an orchard – a peccadillo whose memory he somehow just couldn't throw out. He came to see that that theft had nothing whatever to do with the fact that he was hungry or with the attractiveness of those particular pears. It was really a bid for liberty. He really wanted a certain feeling of freedom and power, of release from the sense of being pressurized and constrained. That was what he wanted – something good, natural, maturing (he was growing up), and spiritual (in the sense of involving his whole self) – not just a pocketful of ripe pears.

He came to see this kind of symbolism in much of his life and to realize that again and again, as his highly sophisticated imagination put it, he had been trying to stop a spiritual itch with the rub of carnal things.

Our view of ourselves can easily be the most inaccurate and mistaken thing about us. Much of it we have received unconsciously from others. We have deduced it from the way they have acted, spoken, looked, in our dealings with them. And that is a very uncertain business. We have a strong tendency to prejudge many of these contacts because of a predisposition (established perhaps very early in our lives) to think cheerfully or gloomily about ourselves.

Freud said 'a man who has been the favourite of his mother keeps for life the feeling of a conqueror'. That could conceivably help him of course, but it might just as easily be a major liability, trapping him forever in adolescence, dooming him to many fouled-up relationships. Its opposite has a similarly deep root and is equally uncertain. Those who are dogged by an obscure tendency to think of themselves as unacceptable for some untraceable reason, and to misinterpret relationships accordingly, are often people who have very mixed memories of their childhood.

Most of us shift rather unsatisfactorily between these two. The mean between the two extremes must be the good fortune of those whose approach to experience is a spiritual one, an approach of the kind of faith that is a basic trust in life. They don't need to be one up on the world very often, and they are not pulled down too far when things go wrong.

We have to admit that some of the truth about ourselves is hidden from us. It's a matter of defences and anxiety-stoppers that we rely on rather a lot but are not yet free enough to challenge. How many husbands and wives, heads of institutions and members of staff, friends and neighbours, could bear to ask each other the question 'But who do *you* say that I am?' and be able to listen to the reply without over-reacting?

When St Paul, dreaming his attractive dream of heaven, said 'then I shall know even as I have been known', it was an intelligent and brave dream he had then. To know oneself without muddle and without protective delusions, to know others without the distortions of the unrealistic demand or the bitter memory, and both within an over-all sanity of compassion learned at the feet of Jesus – well, most of what is partial and incomplete here and now is worth bearing with and working on in the light of a hope as large as that.

The concealed image of oneself is not made up only of the hurts, angers, fears of a long time ago. Within its structure is also the desire for such positive good as is suggested by our intermittent thoughts of God and the meaning of life, our appreciation of the beautiful, and all our desire to help that we may have had to repress for some reason. With most of us there is a fine part of our true self that we have just not allowed to develop, or in some way have devalued and lost touch with.

What I think I am is always much less, much less interesting and hopeful, than what I truly am.

All the more reason for challenging it and enduring the pain of that. Some pain is inevitable. To give up some of my image of what I am, want, deserve, is hard, because I have needed it and used it to protect or console myself. It means a kind of losing face, where 'face' means what I have got into the way of seeing in the mirror of my self-preoccupation. And it needs humility. There is no humility except at the rough hands of humiliation – destruction of supports, exposure to truth, widening of vision.

This must be something of what he meant when he urged people to deny themselves (throw out their redundant and mistaken idea of themselves), accept the pain of that, and follow him in his journey to God.

Ultimately it is only God who can tell us who we are and what we are for. Most of what he says on this topic comes to us through Jesus Christ.

That is why we are Christians. Some people are nervous about using this word of themselves, either because they have an over-moralistic view of what it is to be a Christian or because they are altogether too confused about religious matters.

Most of us are pretty confused. Here are two attractively oblique, nervous, stumbling ways of putting it. One is from the poet W. H. Auden. I think it is just a bit too gloomy, but I like him and his poetry, and I like what he says here. He was the special preacher at a service in Westminster Abbey and in his sermon he said:

> Those of us who have the nerve to call ourselves Christians will do well to be extremely reticent on the subject. Indeed it is almost the definition of a Christian that he is someone who *knows* that he isn't one, either in faith or in morals ... As for loving and forgiving our enemies, the less we say about that the better. Our lack of faith and love are facts we have to acknowledge, but we shall not improve either by morbid and essentially narcissistic moaning over our deficiencies. Let us rather ask, with caution and humour – given our time and place and talents – what, if our faith and

love were perfect, we would be glad to find it obvious to do?[1]

The other is from the great German Catholic theologian Karl Rahner.[2] He wrote of himself as a 'committed' person, by which he meant

> ... a person who hopes that he is a Christian as well as he can manage ... I would like to be a Christian. One has to say 'I would like to be'. In the Christian view one must in the end leave it to God to decide whether one really is, in theory and above all in practice, what one claims to be ... I find that being a Christian is the simplest task, the utterly simple and therefore heavy-light burden, as the gospel calls it ... The longer one lives the heavier and the lighter it becomes. At the end we are left with mystery, but it is the mystery of Jesus.

1. Humphrey Carpenter, *W. H. Auden: A Biography*, Unwin Hyman Ltd 1981, p. 298.
2. Karl Rahner and Karl-Heinz Weger, *Our Christian Faith*, Burns and Oates 1980, pp. 159f., 178.

# 3 Far from the Truth. Two Sons

It's not likely that Jesus had any idea that his words would find a place of gratitude in the minds of the millions who would walk the same earth after him. He just worked his vision of things, the bright and painful substance of his own experience, into all that he so sincerely taught.

But that gave his words such a feel of reality that they have had an unexpectedly contemporary eloquence for every generation. They're always finding us, in the same way as the eyes of a Rembrandt self-portrait seem surprisingly to be following you, looking at you particularly, wherever you move in the gallery.

We can't know how much the story of the two sons (Luke 15.11–32) was his own invention, how much picked out of the mixed currents of the slow deep river of wisdom and tale that flowed through the human mind before books were written; but we certainly can't imagine its interest ever wearing out.

In our time traditional evangelical interpretations of it have lost their old power to reach us and awaken hope, but its psycho-spiritual meanings seem to be winning a new kind of attention, especially when expounded in what may loosely be called Jungian terms, as a dramatic allegory of the way human beings come to terms with reality both within and outside themselves.

There is a sense in which every day somewhere up and down the world a young man gathers all that he has and takes his journey into a far country. It's the old story of finding one's home rather traditional, almost oppressive and suffocating, at any rate incompatible with the dreams and desires stirring now within. In dark moments home can seem a prison.

It's the way God has made us. A time comes when we do genuinely and naturally want to put a distance between ourselves and our parents, and find ourselves, not just be an echo of them.

In many myths and legends there appears the idea of a journey to a far country. The journey, the quest, is sometimes for something lost, sometimes for something not yet found but believed to exist somewhere, though it could be beyond the edge of the world, but it is always in part a quest for full awareness of life and fulfilment of the self.

'"Father, give me the portion of goods that falls to me." And he divided unto them his living.'

We make our journey to reality and maturity with the equipment that falls to us. What has been given us through heredity and natural gifts, through education and learned skills and personal history, together with all the lack, all the absence of this and that which we wish had been given us but wasn't, and all the grief that has come our way, and all the fun – all that, bound up together, makes us what we are when we set out.

If we can manage it, it is good to see all this as mysteriously from God, and to accept it as such, as God's gift to me, a total that's now to be fully employed in this that's to be my life.

That's an important part of living a spiritual life, far more important than prayers, though they may help towards it. It's not easy for anyone, and there are many people for whom to manage it represents nothing less than a victory – because it's as plain as daylight that in this world the equipment for living a decent life has been parcelled out very unequally.

There are always two sides to it. To learn to accept the portion of life's good that has fallen to me involves necessarily learning to accept what did not fall to me. I can't have a different deal now; I may never understand how I came to have this one. For better and worse, this is me; worse, I think,

if I'm on my own, better, so they say, if somehow I push
through to God.

Then comes the young man's experience of how quickly
and efficiently dreams can be destroyed – his inability to get
the hang of his new freedom without idiotic mistakes, the
experience of losing, of losing so much that dependence on
others begins all over again, the menial and humiliating side of
life, the loneliness, the feeling that in this world no one
actually gives anything.

The journey to fulfilment and God involves experiencing
some of all that, and negotiating it, learning from it, acquiring
humanity and understanding from it, registering that we fall
to rise, are baffled to fight better, and that all of us without
exception (the other person maybe particularly) need the
patience and sympathy of others and the merciful help of
God. There is a clue to some help towards this in the
symbolism of 'he sent him into his fields to feed swine'.

It is the fact that they are animals, and not just animals,
since to the Jew they are essentially animals in their unclean-
ness. He has to be with them. He has to look hard and long at
them. He has to smell them. All this he has to experience
almost to the point of identification, till he sees himself as in a
sense one of them, ready, gladly, to eat exactly what they eat.

Coming to the truth about life and God means seeing in a
gutsy way that, as well as being mind and spirit, we are flesh.
Our body with its collection of instinctive reactions and
needs is basically the animal in us.

When we are angry, we in one way or another hit out;
when we are frightened, we withdraw; when we behave
abominably, we are disgusted with ourselves; when we are
lonely, we move towards people. Since this goes for all of us
without exception it is good if we can understand and bear
with one another as these facts are exemplified in this
situation and that. It is ridiculous to think, or act as though
we thought, that we or others are angels.

Most people deny that they ever do so think or act, but the
denial does not seem to be true to the facts.

It is a plausible view that we all have a deep need to believe that, though we ourselves are obviously not holy, at any rate someone is.

Who this someone might be is a bit of a mystery. The odds are, however, that there is some person, some relative or friend, whom we have chosen to bear the projection of this longing, someone whom we need to see as exempt from serious failure, whose fall would not so much evoke our sympathy as be a severe shock to us because it would have broken up an assumption very important to us.

For a number of people this unfortunate character is the priest or minister. He is, of course, the sacred person in their midst, but that is a very different matter from being a holy person. Unfortunately, it is the easiest thing in the world to confuse the sacred and the holy.

And when the priest is seen to fall short of the image thrust on him, the general sense of outrage is intense, a fact which is clearly reflected in the occasional bursts of moral fury in the media. Most people acknowledge how hard it is to forgive. It is particularly hard when the person to be forgiven is someone you have in one way or another privately idolized.

It is equally dangerous in a different way for the victim of your love, especially if this happens to be the priest. Because of how it is within his own human heart, he may derive some obscure security from the role of meeting the world's longing for holiness, and even hide himself from people behind it. The end of that road is his hiding behind it from himself and becoming the one person in the world he never really knows.

It should never be a surprise to us to find that there are other people, as well as ourselves, who are able to deceive, have agonies, want what is not likely to come their way. All without exception have things on their mind and show the strain. Especially those who have thrown in their lot heavily with Jesus have many days when it is a large size in struggles to put faith's dark clichés to the test.

When we have realized these aspects of what it is to be human, realized the shadow side hidden somewhere in it all,

we are ready for a mature relationship with God. In virtue of
that the world can become truly a home for us. The young
man's bit of Jesus's story ends very happily. It makes one
think of T. S. Eliot's line 'Home is where one starts from ..'
and his idea of the circuitous, discovering, yet recognizing
character of growing and maturing:[1]

> We shall not cease from exploration
> And the end of all our exploring
> Will be to arrive where we started
> And know the place for the first time.

In the story, in the middle of the feasting and the dancing is
a man who has truly been through it, come through it, and
come to know life for the first time as home, a place where he
belongs, no longer the stuffy prison it once was but his
father's house, and his.

*       *       *       *       *

His brother ran into difficulties just as costly but at first sight
rather less interesting. When you turn to him you have
certainly left the world of romantic sin. Yet something in
your heart makes you want to signal to him and give some
sign of fellow-feeling.

In family life there is general agreement that certain problems are particularly associated with the first child. There
is sometimes over-carefulness on the part of young and
inexperienced parents. If it is a large family, or a poor one, the
help of the eldest is soon enrolled, there being so much to be
done. Alongside the normal pressures of growing up, the
eldest may have to sustain an excess of parental caution, and
sometimes a too early introduction to the experience of
responsibility.

All these years, he said, he'd served his father and never did
anything anyone could call wrong. That may well have been
the case. Deep inside him, however, he had collected several
resentments, too confused to be properly sorted out – until,

1. T. S. Eliot, 'Little Gidding' from *Four Quartets*, Faber 1944.

perhaps, he himself became a parent and found out how rewarding it all is, and yet how hard, and how easy it is to make mistakes.

Temperamental considerations are important too. Being constitutional, we can't alter them. This man was made of different stuff from his brother in that there was in his emotional life a centripetal tendency, whereas his brother looked outward most of the time.

You could say, then, that some temperamental introversion, maybe, plus perhaps some longstanding inhibiting sense of the burden of responsibility, make this elder brother a man who is unable to take his literal journey into a far country.

When life becomes unbearable for such people they don't get up and clear out, they turn morosely inwards into the labyrinth of the self, where they waste their energy in complaints and thoughts of revenge. Soon they are lost in the loneliness and impoverishment of self-preoccupation, reading baleful significance into other people's meaningless gestures, making issues and grievances out of the small irritations that drop into everyone's life every day, which most people learn to ignore, life being as short and crowded with claims as it is.

This is a more compulsive and lethal condition than the other far country. Such people find it difficult to revise their dark conclusions about life and God and change their self-destructive attitudes and begin to hope again. It is very true to life that this story is open-ended about the elder son. We don't know if he made it, if he ever came back from the waste land in his mind.

What can you do for a man like that? How can you get him out of his gloom and help him to grasp realities and open his eyes? – open them to the surface beauty of life, and the good in people, their admirable tolerances, their amusing foibles, and particularly to the important fact that somewhere in practically everyone's life, though often hidden, there is some sort of a fight going on that they will in fact win if only others will drop their sourness and just try what a bit of affection will do.

Somehow or other he has to be helped to dislodge the thought of *justice* from the moral pedestal on which he has exalted it.

'Lo these many years do I serve thee, neither transgressed I at any time thy commandments' etc., etc. That is to think, and very reasonably, in terms of justice, to argue in the area of the merit and reward principle. It is an admirable principle. We could not run the life of the community without it for one week.

And I'm not going to say that it has no place in the life of a home, because it certainly has.

But a good home is not usually *run* on the principle of merit and reward. Its life is too various and elusive and deep and vivid for that.

It is run on a much looser, more lively, more dangerous principle – of liking and relationship and memory and freedom.

And because it is composed of human beings free to be themselves, free to grow and find their own way to maturity and the truth about things, and none of that is easy, a good home is also necessarily a place of mutual disappointment, a place of hurt, given and received.

And therefore, for it to hold together for more than six months, it just has to be a place of forgiveness.

It has to be a place of forgiveness because some people take longer than others to grow up, and some have more than the usual number of mistakes and foolishnesses to negotiate. And there are some whose service has been taken for granted all these years, and some who just don't happen to excite affection as easily as brighter and more elegant creatures do.

Really there is so much diverse right and wrong in it, so much good luck and bad luck, so much fairness and unfairness, that you have indeed to make forgiveness something of a habit – indeed so much part of the life of the family organism as to become its bloodstream.

When he has come to understand this, however long it takes, and whatever miseries and humiliations he has to go through, the day will arrive, a day of realization, of illumination, when this elder brother also will feel that he has come an incredible distance, from a very far country, and arrived where he started, and now knows the place for the first time, as his home.

# 4 Absent God. Providence

We are never in fact alone. Our loves may die, our friends leave us for more interesting companions, and even the love that lasts through to the end carries a core of solitude; but God stays with us whatever happens. He is always the present one.

When, as he died, our Lord cried out that he had been abandoned by God (Matt. 27.46), he was expressing his sense of desolation, but the truth was all the other way. He was not left to his fate.

It is the Christian view, and there is hardly a more important thought in the whole of the Christian view of life, that, far from being absent, God was supremely present with Jesus at the great public, sacrificial, revelatory climax of his driven life.

In times of physical and emotional crisis, what we have so far come to believe about God may well go under for a while; but however sharp the sense of God's absence, we believe that to be a mistaken interpretation. God is always there. Though I make my bed in hell, behold thou art there.

Even if we can't believe that for the time being, the substance of our faith still remains. The sense of being abandoned does not necessarily mean loss of faith, though it may well mean faith shaking in fear. It happens again and again *within* faith, as it did with Jesus. His cry of desolation made clear, not the break-up of his faith, but the persisting relationship with God that provoked the cry, survived the terror from which it was flung out into space, and made

possible the last gift of himself to the Father that has made the
world think new thoughts about death ever since.

God is never absent. But the thought of his presence is one
that needs to be looked over and unpacked much more than is
usually done in Christian conversation.

We are normally inclined to associate the presence of God
with all life's lift and encouragement. The beauty of the
world, the love of friends (and maybe 'one especial'), the
interest of the search for truth in anything and everything,
progress, healings, happinesses, successes – it is natural for a
Christian to interpret these spiritually and see them as flames
of the true fire that is the light of the world.

Unfortunately, by some perverse logic, this seems to
condition us to register our disappointments, unhealed sick-
nesses, guilts, as God's absence. That is to misunderstand life.
God is present quite as much in the darkness as he is in the
light; according to the Bible they are all the same to him.

They are not really all the same to us. As time goes on we
do seem to learn more, grow and deepen as human beings
more, through our struggles than our thrills. Under some
pain, it is true, we may collapse, and afterwards have to start
re-building a self that can trust and be generous again.
However, while certain of life's normally critical periods of
growth, like adolescence, first love, early years of marriage,
the mid-life challenges, and the coping with loss, success,
humiliation, are all associated with the heart's darkness and
pain, it is through such important struggles that we move
forward. By 'moving forward' I mean growing in self-
understanding, compassion, generous appreciation of life and
competence at living it.

God's presence does not come and go. All the time,
whatever the emotional weather, his presence is the constant,
while our registering of it, our interpretation of it, is the
variable.

Sometimes it is marvellous, and sometimes it is dreadful.
When we are in the wrong and are not doing anything about
bringing rightness into the situation, God's presence with us

is in fact those feelings of unease and dissatisfaction that are making us miserable.

They all have an essentially positive function, as God's presence always has, in that they are there to stimulate appropriate thought and action and bring us into the light again.

That's just an example. In this region of the spiritual life, guilt is no different from other forms of unrest not associated with blame, like fear, doubt, and various types of conflict. They all represent the presence of God as wanting us to make some step forward or let something go or re-direct part of our energy that is being wasted in mistaken use – and we are resisting or frightened and consequently having a struggle with ourselves. But God's nearness is not in question; you can't be much nearer to God than when you're fighting him.

Some time ago I had a remarkable dream. It was a complicated affair but I managed to recall most of it on waking and write it down. The later part of it involved a huge crowd of people in India, thousands of them swaying and dancing in some kind of religious festival, a beating of drums in the rear, and a sort of anxiety lest all this should get out of hand.

A very small Malaysian man, barefoot, ran out in front of them, in a sense leading them (he might have been a child) and proclaiming again and again 'Cling to God not as God but as sorrow!' I found this exhortation intensely illuminating, and I felt that it meant that anyone who wants God should look at the negative features of his or her life. It is there that God is for that person.

I felt that there is some link between this utterance and the Beatitudes. Just as this incantatory plea pointed to the presence of God not in some light beyond us but in some shadow within, so the Beatitudes suggest a blessedness in being poor, hungry, grieving, injured. I woke with a kind of wondering joy, feeling that, as far as my ignorant life was concerned, a fresh insight into the meaning of things had been given me.

When we think God is unreal it is worth while trying to

find out from ourselves what we imagine his real presence would be like. We must then ask if we are sure that that must be the only form it could take. Could we not cling to God not as God but as hidden in the unreality or pain that just now is wearing us down?

*     *     *     *     *

When I was doing hospital chaplaincy I frequently found myself listening to the complaint 'Why should this happen to me?' – more often from men than from women, though I don't know if there is any evidence for its being a particularly masculine reaction to illness. A Roman Catholic colleague in the chaplaincy often used to ask such a patient, in the kindest possible way, who he thought it ought to have happened to.

Behind it, whether expressed or not, is the assumption that misfortune is normally to be traced to some moral inadequacy and that this is not true of my case. Whatever my failures have been, and nobody is perfect, the justice of things doesn't warrant my being made to bear this.

It is something of a mystery where people learn this moralistic view and the idea of a punishing God that usually goes with it.

The Bible is partly responsible. While there is much biblical teaching of the opposite kind (especially in the book of Job and some of the words of Jesus), there is certainly in the Old Testament quite enough of the idea that those who do that which is evil in the sight of the Lord come to a very sticky conclusion to set people's minds going along this unhelpful path.

However, I don't think that's the main source of the idea. People adopt it who have never had any religious instruction, bad or good, as well as some who think religion is a load of rubbish.

The idea is, I believe, an extrapolation from childhood experience. There are people who grew up in a demanding and critical atmosphere in which misdemeanours were met unfailingly with punishment or at any rate the obvious withdrawal of parental love. Even in intelligent and happy homes the most reasonable kind of early teaching about behaviour is bound to deposit in the child's mind the association of misbehaviour with parental disapproval.

In normal moral development this association gives way to more mature and complex reasoning. But there are many people who have had little chance of developing their ideas of the why and wherefore of things, of the way some things don't tie up one with another and some unexpectedly do.

Accordingly their tendency as adults is unconsciously to transfer their childhood thoughts about their parents to the anonymous flow of life. So when life turns against them and they can't explain its unfriendliness by recalling some evidence of their somewhere, some time, breaking the rules, it all seems unjust – 'why pick on me?'

They would find it a great help if they could abandon this much-worn mental route, cast a cold eye on things and see that evil annoyingly falls on the good as well as the not so good with the same impartiality as that shown by the light of the sun. Goodness doesn't entail success any more than badness entails inevitable penalty. If people will recognize that life is sometimes logical, at other times apparently quite illogical, but always a risky affair for all of us, they will be all the freer to make something of its magnificence and pain.

It's also worth pointing out that the question 'why me?' is one we rarely ask about our good fortune and the days when things go very well indeed. It's only when things go wrong that we feel we have been singled out unfairly to confront the size of life and the fierceness of its face.

Happiness has as much mystery about it as suffering, and in certain singularly fresh and attractive minds (like Thomas Traherne for example) can provoke its own incredulous 'why me?' The capacity for that kind of delighted surprise is one of the gifts of a spiritual life.

I am sure that many people want rather more consolation than this seems to offer. I have never in my life thought of religion as being in the consolation trade. Why should the idea of God always console? If it did I would immediately suspect it as projection of human wishes and a sign of world-weariness. I think 'God the great consoler' is yet one more idea of him to be jettisoned.

Of course, the boat of faith will rock more, but the voyage will be more interesting. It's quite marvellous the freshness that can come into life not from finding some new truth but simply from scrapping a belief that won't bear examination, that you've been ill at ease with for quite some time.

There are lots of these beliefs about – like 'I can't believe in a God who allows x, y, z, etc'. Who, with any authority, ever said that a God worthy of human belief would of course not allow x, y, z? Some people don't want God, they just want a good-looking teddy-bear. Isn't it part of God's outrageous interest, part of the *mysterium tremendum*, that he does in fact allow x, y, z, and we can't see why?

# 5 Possessing and Giving

Religion can never be perfectly clear. Von Hügel said that when it was made clear to him he became uneasy. 'I feel it's a fake. I know I've left something out.'

Institutional religion seems geared mostly to minds under fourteen years of age. When that bit of your youth is behind you, you begin to find religion rather irritating. It's mainly because your mind is stirring. You want answers, not nativity plays for the children. You certainly want clarity.

Adult religion begins exactly there. It begins with disappointment, with the realization that little of Christian faith is going to be obvious, that from now on, and for good, you're going to be coping with the unclear statement and the dusty answer.

As an example, I think of his devastating advice, 'Sell what you have and give to the poor, and you will have treasure in heaven; and come, follow me' (Mark 10.17–23).

He was talking to an exceptional individual. Most of us would think that if we had lots of money and no guilts we would be happy enough. Not this man apparently. He had problems. His main worry was that good thing believed to be on the far side of death. How does one make sure of it? If we knew how to make sure of it, it would make death look quite small. Death is a bitter thought to a man living at peace among his possessions.

I don't think Jesus told him. That was not his style. He didn't give answers. This may have been because he thought the answers have to come from us.

Nor did he give him a load of advice that was too radical by half.

He just set up a kind of spiritual ferment in the man, which he was going to have to bear with, struggle with, work through for the rest of his days.

The implication was that so doing he would either find his question answered or realize that it was unanswerable.

'Sell what you have and give to the poor.' It was an extraordinary thing to say to a generous and good man. There must have been many people who had that man to thank for their taste of the goodness of life, the unexpected light on the black day, the cancelled debt. Jesus didn't urge him to do just a bit more of that.

He presented him dramatically with the vision of a total detachment from *all* he had, in face of the infinite need of a suffering world.

What can you do with that? All you can do with it is live with it and see what happens.

A lot of people are trying to live with it, and finding it almost unbearable.

We just have to bear it if we are determined to live and not hide. It's easier to hide. You don't have to be a Christian to realize that there's too much hiding going on, but Christians are likely to be particularly uncomfortable about it.

Here in the West most Christians find that we are living the more or less comfortable life of the Western bourgeoisie in a world full of outrageous imbalances, a world of famine, local wars (often armed by the great powers), miserable under-development, and so on. The Christian with money to spend leafing through the latest catalogue of video equipment or home computers or continental holidays is doing that in a world in which half the population want and need a decent meal more than anything else. Has one the Christian right to own even a television set in such a world?

Our emotions can get into the most gigantic turmoil with such self-questioning. What exactly is the use of such periodic attacks of ineffectual conscience is difficult to say, but that doesn't alter the fact that a lot of people who truly want God are seriously troubled about this.

It has dogged Christian footsteps from the very beginning. It's the classic tension between inadequate commitment to Christ and scrupulosity. It seems we either live in a false and discreditable peace of mind or we paralyse our life with neurotic perfectionism.

The struggle to cope with this is an important form of meditation.

It becomes clear at once that you can't live a life of endless self-questioning. You'll never get anything done.

There's a further danger. One of the perils of the scrupulous life is that in itself it can be an escape. Scrupulous anxiety often turns out to be an evasion of some single personal issue whose importance is obscured by exaggerated attention to more distant and more arguable points of behaviour.

There is also a hidden vanity to be taken into account. The scrupulous, perhaps unconsciously, are often seeking an esoteric satisfaction of their egos. They attempt to measure up to an idealized Christian image of the self while being unaware that this spiritual athleticism is a defence against the humiliation of acknowledging one's failures and realizing with a natural sadness that we are all sinners.

And once again we are brought up against the truth that we are never going to have it all clear. It is a painful business consorting with Jesus. He plasters his irritating questionmark over everything we call our own. Do you really want this? Do you need that? And this other thing, couldn't you let go of such a small thing for heaven's sake?

He is a disturbing friend. He used the word 'friend' about us, and it is something we have always found attractive; but we would never take from a human friend what comes from him. Perhaps 'friend' is one of the many inappropriate pietistic words.

However, there must be something wrong if deciding for him makes us miserable. In this story we are told that Jesus looked at this man with love. It's an appealing touch.

References to the affectionate side of Jesus's personality are not all that common in the New Testament. It's good to have this one.

Perhaps Jesus loved him because he was a man who really had done a great deal for God. 'All these have I observed from my youth.' Every intelligent, reasonable, devout Jew would say 'All right; that's enough; our fathers in the faith have always said that that's enough. That is absolutely certain to bring you the eternal life that is God's promise to Israel. What are you worrying about?'

Yet there's no doubt that he was worried. And perhaps it was that that melted Jesus's heart.

Jesus himself, it seems, had paced around in that night of the soul in which the virtuous wonder if what they have managed to observe of God's will is in fact enough. It looks as if he did not feel he had done enough. 'Why do you call me good? No one is good, save God.'

There may have been another issue altogether – that this man had done enough but there is nevertheless an unpleasant hollowness at the heart of the most complete moral achievement. If he had come up against that particular emptiness he would know that goodness doesn't deliver the spiritual thing most people are wanting.

Jesus knew it too; and he had discovered it the same hard way, that's to say, not our way but the hard way, by being truly good and doing good and finding the subtle disappointment that can lie at the centre of all that. He could have felt that this man was a twin soul, one of his own kind. There would be a world of meaning in the way he looked on him and loved him.

Jesus was a lot younger than most of us. We've had much longer on the road but obviously know less about it than he did. He looked at everyone the same way, looking beyond your eyes and mouth into your life – as if there was one thing he would be excited to find there, some word, sigh, fierceness, sadness that reveals the presence of the spiritual. He knew it is somewhere in everyone.

Uncertainty and difficulty are an important part of the spiritual dimension. There are some matters of behaviour and belief about which we shall be in doubt all the way until paradise. It's been said that the devil is the absence of doubt. At the same time, anyone trying to live a spiritual life is wise to keep feeding into the imagination one conviction that is not in doubt at all. As a result of many mistakes and not a little pain, it has been deeply etched on the Christian mind that it is always the apprehension of good that makes spiritual progress possible, not the anxious attempt to avoid evil. God, and the goodness of life, and acts of love whenever we can get around to doing some of them – these normally should determine the general tone of the mind. The happier we are the sooner will our hold loosen on satisfactions that perplex us. Anxiety merely makes that hold the more rigid and compulsive.

So Jesus's reply to this man who is finding death looking larger as it moves nearer is to put before him the mystery of the world's immense poverty, its infinite hunger for all that materially and spiritually makes life worth living. The implication is that in face of that colossal lack, that void stretching half across the world, all that you at this moment have begins to look embarrassing and expendable. Compassion does a marvellous work of liberation, even from worry about death and what lies beyond it.

And to the man's confusion of question and excitement he continues 'And come, follow me.'

Once you have seen the vast incalculable need of the world and stopped yourself looking the other way and felt your hold on what you possess loosen, you will probably have to take another step.

You can't bear all that on your own. You can't live simply and solely in terms of the world's need. To see it large is one thing, is a good thing. To make it the absolute, to see nothing else, will finish you and any usefulness you could be to the world.

There is, however, this man Jesus, who is living all the time virtually in sight of the kingdom of God, of the coming fullness of life, the justice and peace that he says are promised to the world. And there is his call to come and learn with him what that vision means, and how what we do with what we have can fit into it and be made part of its realization.

To respond to his call is not to make sure of eternal life. Eternal life is not something you can make sure of inheriting, as though giving to the poor and following Jesus are what you put down for your ticket to paradise.

Eternal life – all we can ever possibly know about it – is in fact the life of compassion and faith (life in God) here and now, and the hope that this will see us through when there seems to be no place beyond here for us and no time beyond now.

# 6 Making it Worth While

Two of his friends once asked Jesus if he could make following him worth their while in the end. That was what they were after, but they used religious, metaphorical language for it, about sitting on his right hand and on his left in his 'glory' (Mark 10.35–40).

He replied 'what you want is not mine to give'; and he added, somewhat inconsequentially, 'it is for those for whom it has been prepared.'

He may have been dismissing the whole idea with an oracular, ambiguous statement like 'in heaven we shall get what is waiting for us there'.

Whether this helps or not, it's significant, in some way that may take a bit of digging out, that St John's Gospel likes to think of the cross as Jesus's 'glory'.

On his right hand and on his left there he had two thieves.

It's quite clear, however, that there are some things he can't give – not because he is withholding them for some reason but because he in fact hasn't got them, to give or deny us.

And one of them has to do with one-upmanship and doing well, being seen to have made the right choices and to be on the winning side.

It's not that Jesus was against success and the successful, that he for some obscure reason sided with life's failures. Only a fool would do that. It's simply that he lived in the kind of mental world where winning and losing have a very different look from that which thrills or dismays most of us, and indeed all of us most of the time.

We usually begin our Christian life at some point or other in our second or third decades. It doesn't matter whether we are marvellously or only modestly equipped with what it takes to make a go of life, whether we had a fortunate or a troubled childhood, the self that we offer to life in the name of Christ is already a wounded thing.

No one is ever allowed to grow up evenly in this world, unfolding smoothly like a flower from bud to bloom, his individual needs satisfactorily met, his personal possibilities revealed and given scope in a happy maturing process. For various reasons, some of them now not traceable, in our early years some of our needs were certainly not met, some of our potential was not drawn out and given its chance.

Consequently, some of the small crises and disappointments of life, that ordinarily provide the healthy and invigorating friction our spiritual self needs in order to grow, became for us threatening situations we did not negotiate very successfully. Our competence and confidence took certain knocks, which in turn made it certain that they would have to take more.

The result is that in each one of us, behind what everyone else sees, just under the surface, sometimes exposed but always there, is inevitably a certain amount of anxiousness, of feeling isolated in a potentially hostile world.

The other side of that coin is naturally the desire for that which will assuage it, allay it and give us the relief of feeling more secure, through whatever bits of power and success we can pick up from day to day. One moves towards or clings to whoever seems in one way or another prestigious and influential. Friendships, associations, interests may all be subtly threaded on the string of 'glory for me'. Even our religion may be a clinging thing rather than the loving we would like it to be.

We are usually quite unaware that this is to a considerable extent what makes us tick. It is part of the spiritual life that that desire needs to be unearthed and shown that it is not going to get what it wants, at any rate from religion.

It's true that whatever talent and good fortune we have, and the hard work we put in, may indeed bring us some success and the sense that it's all been worth it; but that sort of thing we are not going to get from following Christ. He hasn't anything like that to give.

In the kingdom of God (which is a way of saying 'ultimately') what you get, what is granted, is part of God's eternal purpose. It has been prepared from the beginning. It is not alterable as a result of human requests, whether they are prayers or attempts at bargaining or just sighs. It is what has always been and is always the case.

From the very beginning God has offered us himself. That means, in this world, whatever knowledge of his love we can take, some understanding of his will for us, some awareness of his presence in the good and ill of life, some spiritual joy, and some share in the pain of it all.

You don't get that by asking for it. You get it by faith and hope and love, which is the only way to learn life's truth and to release our innate capacity to rejoice in it. It is also the only way to realize that ultimately all that is corrupt and broken, all that is outraged, will be found to be no more than provisional when the glory of the Lord shall be revealed and all flesh shall see it together.

# 7 Time. The Present Moment

In the New Testament world there are two ideas of time. There is 'chronos', which is clock-time, time as it passes, the fleetingness that is always taking day into night in order to bring on yet another but different day. Chronos is the continual disappearance in which the lives we live are soaked. All experience, to the reflecting mind, has an elegiac note, because to realize with delight, love, relief, something that is happening to us means that it is already slightly in the past, has begun to move away, and we are to some extent looking back, reflecting on it.

It's not everyone who hears this elegiac note in things, but many do – many poets, whole regional mentalities like the Welsh and Slav peoples, and certainly Jesus did. His images of the moth and rust havoc in all that we try to lay in for keeps, of the beating flood and wind that test whatever we build, of the chance that's around for only a time and is missed by those who come too late, his sense that the children of chronos are necessarily children of sadness because everything is passing away except ... these images impress him on our minds as a man who felt substance leaking drop by drop from the unsafe vessel of this world. He was able to bear all that because he knew something else.

The other idea of time in the New Testament is 'kairos', which is time plus meaning, time plus importance, time that's not just two hands on a clock or some sterile digital thing, but an inner moment of insight and opportunity. Particularly it is time as that through which the eternal (the eternal truth, life, love) comes and speaks and takes what would be otherwise our flimsy mortal beings into his everlasting arms.

Jesus often spoke about this moment that can come any time, often unexpectedly, swollen with the great kingdom of God in it. He lived in expectancy, always feeling that in some way now is the hour one has been waiting for.

It happens with us too. When you are in some dilemma, wondering what on earth to do, quite floundering, it often happens that suddenly he is there, at your elbow, saying something you've heard the church say infinitely boringly a hundred times but now at last he is saying it at the right time, and you hear.

*   *   *   *   *

When the will of God doesn't get done in this world it's as much because it comes up against human anxiety as through being blocked by human sin. Anxiety persists hauntingly in many lives, continually looking for new forms in which to appear with its harassed face. If there are not enough fears in my life, it will invent some for me, or just settle for pulling out some old wound from the past to mess up any tranquillity I may have found.

Jesus was a practical, one item at a time man, with no admiration at all for minds that rush ahead. He seemed to think that there is enough bad, and good, in any one day for us to be able conscientiously to call it a day as it fades around us in the evening.

In the huge pile of stuff that is recommended to Christians for spiritual reading I have not found anyone who so clearly and practically interpreted this part of his teaching as J.P. de Caussade in his thoughts on the sacrament of the present moment.

It is part of that idea that if the present is not exactly wonderful for you, then it's worth finding out why, finding out whether or not there is a problem at this moment, and, if there is one, doing now whatever can be done about it now. If there isn't any problem just now, then there's nothing to stop us looking around to see if there isn't on the contrary something to be enjoyed, and simply enjoying it.

There are naturally many huge problems and needs about which Jesus hasn't one single word for us, and we grope on in the dark or in whatever light we find from other sources. But his teaching about living in the present goes a remarkably long way into things.

It's the inner note of his endless obsession with the kingdom of God. The word 'present' has both temporal and spatial meanings in its resonance.

Whatever is present is in front of me now; it is also impermanently there; being momentary, it is fading, and it must pass away sooner or later.

Doing the will of God means accepting this in the depths of one's heart. It is wise to think of happiness not in terms of just one situation or one emotional condition. That is to become a nervously clutching or a dreamily restless individual.

If the desired situation is with me now, it is, even so, time-driven. To live intelligently means to be ready, even if it is mostly at some great depth of being, for it to go.

If it is not with me yet, let that be so too. I must let it not be yet. It's possible to use up all your days seeing happiness mistily in the future, unaware that you are always sure to see some blemish on what is present because your faith is that somewhere else is nearer the centre of joy. In time I shall be a happier person, not so given to obscure refusals and withdrawals, better adjusted altogether, genuinely loving God, not trying to make out that I do.

God is the universally present one. It's a belief that is at the centre of many religions. The present moment is always his presence. His presence is always the present moment. The present moment invariably consists principally in something to be done or something to be put up with or something to be enjoyed. Attending wholeheartedly to whichever of these is the case is what is meant by responding to God and doing his will.

\* \* \* \* \*

You say 'I'm not asking for *feelings*. What I can't cope with is the sense of the appalling unreality of it all.'

The sense of unreality can descend at any time and in any area of life. There's always the possibility that some personal pre-occupation, or some barely conscious mix of memory and desire, is making life's daily claims and interests fade.

Even so, one job that has to be done, and frequently re-done is to rescue God from the narrowness of our spiritual programme – what we do to express and stimulate our spiritual self. You can't put the whole of yourself into the same programme year in year out. When you can't give your whole self to it, it, whatever it is, is bound to seem increasingly unreal.

When you speak about the unreality of it all, I wonder what 'it' is. If it is God, then I want to ask how does anyone register the reality of God?

I know that you are fond of *The Cloud of Unknowing*. Surely the teaching in that marvellous book puts a question-mark over the search for 'reality' in the experience of God. In this it is far more contemporary for us than many of the ancient texts and many modern ones too.

God is not an item in the universe that can be identified and known in himself. You can say what you think he isn't, but your shots at saying what he is will be less successful because he is bound to be infinitely more than what you say of him. Words drawn from human life, like 'father' (though Jesus seemed to be able to use that word all the time), have for us only a limited value when applied to God. No father would allow his children to suffer what humanity has to suffer. Soon all our words fade, lose any meaning they ever had, in a kind of cloud of ignorance.

That obscurity and incomprehensibility will always be there, between our minds and God. All we have in this life is longing and love, and resentment and gratitude, and question and complaint, and gratitude again.

I don't think we can ever *know* that we know God. We can't *know* that we have found him, or for that matter haven't found him. There are some encouraging voices. Think of Pascal's 'console yourself: you would not seek me if you had not already found me'.

You can't say that he is 'real' in some dark moody music of late Schubert, or in someone's quite bewildering love for you, but non-existent in some tatty religious service. You can talk about the satisfaction and peace to be found in some experiences and the depressing inadequacies of others; but if we are going to use God-language I think we must say that we believe he is in all three experiences, indeed in all experiences, but saying different things.

What he says in our experiences of life's unreality, pain, mystery, is often hard to hear or to bear; but to those who go on with the longing and the loving it seems to become audible and bearable. Sometimes it leads us into a quite new depth of faith where such experiences begin to look as if they give us far more than they deny us or take from us.

When we can't cope with the unreality or the pain, it's good to make clear to ourselves that it is, after all, God with whom we can't cope, that we shall probably with his help get round to coping eventually, and that meanwhile we might try being still and silent and allowing some of the sense of the great wholeness of life to come back.

In that whole, we have told ourselves time and time again, much proclaims him. Our great and small experiences of life's goodness have turned us to him, our awareness of its frightful miseries is our awareness of its cry for a saviour, and its monotonies of routine and loneliness and triviality make us think of those whose lives are nothing but that emptiness, and we hate the thought that they should die with all their aspiration and love unused, ignored, even laughed at by some bitter fool. Is there not something we can do?

In Becket's *Waiting for Godot*[1] there is a point where the two tramps keep hearing blind Pozzo calling for help. One of them says:

---

1. Samuel Beckett, *Waiting for Godot*, Faber 1962, p.79.

Let us not waste our time in idle discourse! Let us do something, while we have the chance! It is not every day that we are needed. Not indeed that we personally are needed. Others would meet the case equally well, if not better. To all mankind they were addressed, those cries for help still ringing in our ears! But at this place, at this moment of time, all mankind is us, whether we like it or not. Let us make the most of it, before it is too late!

# 8 Holiness, Self-Denial, Growth

If you are trying to find out what it means to see first the kingdom of God, and do that thing, you are likely to find the idea of holiness rather less than illuminating. It is so tantalizingly undefined in Christianity. The examples of it which the church has selected from the Christian millions to arouse our pride in their company and inspire our flagging commitment – I mean the saints – lead one to think that historically holiness has been found mainly in priests, religious, people who have done some notable social work, and especially sufferers of one kind and another.

If you look through the calendar of saints you will not find many politicians, scientists, artists, scholars, prisoners of conscience, and few people who were admirable simply because they did something that is certainly wonderful and incalculably important – were mothers and fathers of understanding, imagination, patience, happiness. Generally speaking it is secular opinion and gratitude that have asked us to look at these and be glad and give thanks.

If it is right to single out people and give them marks for holiness, when I think of a man like Henry James, his sheer goodness and the volume of splendid work he produced and left to adorn what remains of time, some of the so-called saints, as far as we can see through the haze of the past, look suspiciously like immature and even disturbed human beings.

I particularly wish that the church had taken more notice of artists, of all the kinds there are. Cesare Pavese spoke of artists as the monks of the bourgeois state. In them the common man

may see the life of contact with the eternal that the peasants of
the Middle Ages saw in the friars. To my mind, that may be a
bit of an exaggeration, but it's a very congenial one.

The church has certainly engaged the artist's talent and gift
– in the building of the great cathedrals, in the vast body of
painting and music provided by creative genius for the
worship and contemplation of Christian minds; but it does
not often honour them verbally in its prayer and praise. On
the whole Christian thankfulness is a moralistic and un-
aesthetic thing.

*    *    *    *    *

I've been looking at a new dictionary of spirituality. Partly
because it was the end of the day and I was tired, partly
because at this time of the year and in the last of the day's
light the garden has a wan and exhausted look, I was not
much cheered by it.

We can presume that all these names refer to individuals
who each knew some partial aspect of the name that is above
every name. Yet reading about them, assembled prestigiously
together in this large book, I found myself surprised that the
ultimate has been so familiar to so many people, an almost
common experience it seems, while my own knowledge of it
seems so insignificant.

The mistake there, and perhaps it's one that dictionaries of
spirituality encourage you to make, is in thinking of God in
terms of the exceptional.

Religion is really like the air you breathe and the food you
eat, something basic you live on and don't think about with
any solemnity most of the time, indeed often take for granted;
yet at the same time it's something as momentous as truth,
without which we can't sort out anything that matters and
life amounts to little more than the blind busyness of the ant-
heap or a frenetic day in the stock exchange.

Even such high-toned, perhaps slightly hysterical, thoughts
can't be with you all the time. All the things that make up the
average ordinary day don't seem to have much to do with
faith while you are doing them. They're just your life, what

you have to get done because it's Wednesday, or Thursday, however much you long for a bit of a change and for God to appear from behind the cloud of unknowing where he spends the major part of his time.

It's part of the Christian idea that the other world surrounds us always. We're living in it all the time. God is never to be thought of as at the end of some pilgrimage or search or as a reality that will come to you powerfully when you get around to serving life as it deserves.

His reality is so close that you can't distinguish it from what you just have to get done because it's Wednesday. You can't be aware of him (in the normal sense of being aware) most of the time. We become aware of him in that sense mainly by memory and reflection.

He is rather like happiness. Happiness doesn't tell you all there is to know about God, but it takes you part of the way. It's a marker. We can't grasp it and live it and at the same time know that we have it. As soon as I *know*, as soon as I say 'How happy I am!', the immediacy has gone from the experience, I have slipped away from it, put a bit of distance between myself and the enjoying or the loving (whatever it is), and turned it into an object I can look at, reflect on; and then it must necessarily begin to fade.

'By love he may be gotten and held; by thought never.' You can *be* a moment of happiness, so that 'you are the music while the music lasts', but to *know* that must mean that you have extricated yourself from the happiness somewhat, in order to observe it. All you will then see is the gleam of its retreating edge. We are so made that, as God was concerned with great tenderness to explain to Moses, we are not in this world going to be able to see God's face – only gaze on his retreating back as he leaves.

*   *   *   *   *

The saying about denying oneself, taking up one's cross and following him, is only doubtfully one of the sayings of Jesus (Mark 8.34). It was probably set later among his remembered words as an encouragement and stiffener for persecuted

Christians now finding the way unbearable. We can think of
them as the words of the Christ of faith to the Christians of
history.

Mistaken interpretations of the saying have had a forceful
role in the development of some Christian ideas of the
spiritual life. Their unsatisfactoriness has been exposed
in many twentieth-century consulting-rooms, and indeed
wherever one beleaguered soul has tried to help another.

Many people whose emotions have got into a dark turmoil
have been helped into the light again by being encouraged to
acknowledge how much they have unhelpfully denied themselves, in the sense of denying how things actually were with
them, or refusing a voice to what in them had a right to be
heard.

Things began to come straight again when, for example,
they stopped denying the place that a certain anger was
holding in their lives or refusing a glance at the hidden love or
smothered despair that was behind their fatigue. And this
meant no longer denying themselves some interest in the
inner world of their feelings.

Turning off that form of self-denial is the first step towards
understanding oneself. The journey into self-understanding is
as necessary as any, even though we never come to the end of
it. Whatever we are to other people, we shall always be a bit
of a mystery to ourselves, and every so often we shall wonder
why we did such a thing or felt like that.

There's a providence in the mystery of personality. The
interest of it is stimulating. There may be some kind of
protection too in the fact that no one on earth can read us like
a book, not even ourselves. It's not likely that we could cope
with the full view. The full view of what I am is something
only God has; but in the end I shall share it with him. I shall
be able and I shall be ready to know even as I have been
known.

While we realize that there is no spiritual growth without
growth in self-understanding, what we are growing *into* is not
so clear. We believe we know the general direction, the way.

We would not be helped by knowing more. He didn't set himself up as a model. He preferred to talk of himself as a way, the true way, of going about the business of life. He may have meant no more than that he trusted that what he thought and felt so deeply was of the truth.

The Bible does as a matter of fact play with the idea of a model, but it has a useful vagueness. We are created to be something not quite seen or understood, called the stature of Christ.

It's interesting that that image, the image of the man Jesus, so tremendously Jewish and daunting and merciful and impatient with this world, so certain of something that redeems life from its infuriating relativity, its inability ever to come to a conclusion or give an answer – that image, or something very like it, seems to be secretly wanted by most of the world, yet its outline is always a little blurred.

One clue he gave was, as a recommendation for the meditating mind, what it is to be a child. I think he meant a child not as some kind of goal that we must reach (that would be putting things the wrong way round) but as a symbol of growth.

Every child is a being in transit, growing up and, normally, wanting to grow up. Children are rarely found playing with other children at being children, almost always at being adults. That is their being's direction.

At the same time every child is in fact a child, with impulses not yet organized in coherence, any one of which can suddenly become too much for him and steal the show. And he might well be overwhelmed entirely if he hadn't the refuge of home and family, where he is loved not for his successes but for himself. So, after his failures in the business of growing up he can withdraw, until his emotional storm dies down and his zest for life shines through again like the sun after a shower.

This is always our inner situation. It is never superseded. Whatever St Paul meant by what he said in 1 Corinthians 13, we never 'put away' the child in us; or if we do, if we repress our awareness of that part of us, we are in for trouble. All the time, part of us is wanting to grow and part is finding it just a bit beyond us.

André Malraux said that a priest told him that hearing confessions had taught him two things – that people are much more unhappy than we think, and that there is no such thing as a grown-up person. Well, 'no such thing as a grown-up person' in the sense of a person who has finally put away childish things, certainly. The point is that no such person has ever existed or could exist. We are always beings in the process of growing up, with some new range of experience and ability developing and some immaturity in us slowing things down.

Accepting God as a little child must mean accepting one's essential human condition, of growing and yet not being quite ready, of wanting to move forward and yet resisting too. And it should mean being decent to oneself about this, not patronizing, or rigorist, or sentimental.

People feel the tension of it in a hundred different ways. One very common one is in learning how to wait 'and not be tired by waiting'. For the sake of some present interest or some good in the future the expression of some feelings and the gratification of some wishes just have to be deferred. Such postponement is disliked by children, but it's just as painful later, in all the human waiting for love, for freedom, for a bit of peace. Someone has said that Judas betrayed Jesus not because he was his enemy; he was his dear friend and believed in his coming victory, but so much that he couldn't wait for it and was driven to attempt to hasten it by forcing Jesus's hand, only to see everything go terribly wrong.

The undertow of the child in us is felt too in the difficulty of relating feelings to situations sensibly. Children are not so good at this. And we certainly don't want them to be very good at it. It's different with us. The honest expression of feeling is good; it's better still if it's not in excess of the facts.

Many resentments and fears and much sentimentality represent a fuller flow of feeling than the situation warrants. If this happens frequently with us it usually means that some resentment, fear, love, related to some other experience (which indeed we may have forgotten) that has not yet found appropriate expression, has burst through to fire up the emotion naturally stirred by the current situation.

The sentimental film doesn't really deserve so many tears, the annoyance, the overheard remark, doesn't warrant quite so much anger and sense of humiliation. All of us have a supply of unexpressed feeling which, given its chance, will burst through and make us look ridiculous or behave badly, even make a complete wreck of things. It's part of the human condition of both child and adult. It doesn't change just because we've stacked up a few years.

A spiritually alive person is aware of the ebb and flow of feeling, and of the unfathomableness of some of it. We have to try to get as much of ourself as possible expressed in our ordinary living, to be kind towards the self that must have a poor deal just now because of circumstances, and to spot hangovers from the past that haven't much relevance today.

A very wide range of experience opens up before the growing human being as a result of increasing rationality and emotional freedom. Trust and anger become possible to him each in its appropriate place, a sensible level of expectation (many kinds of goods are available), the readiness to enjoy credit and take blame. He comes to be able to make use of criticism, usually hurt by it of course but not often completely floored. And around him there is the huge world of other people and their enthusiasms, insights, pains, calling to him to come on in and lend a hand, to have a look at this and that – all the incalculable world of significant living.

All this existential situation is particularly easy to see in the vivid growing of a child: which is why Christianity urges us to receive the kingdom of heaven in terms of that fascinating, forward looking being, whose complicated soul faces, sometimes inconveniently, two ways.

# BELIEVING AND LOVING

# 1 Spirituality Today. The Word 'God'. Preaching

The other day I saw a definition of religion as 'whatever we do to come to grips with the questions that confront us when we realize that we, and others like us, are alive in this sort of a world, and that we will die'. An interesting conversation could certainly start there; but very soon one awkward point would probably be made by someone.

There are many people who are just not confronted with any questions of a general nature, even on a wet day, least of all questions about life and death. Life and death are beautiful and sonorous words in many literary contexts but rather intimidating when looked in the eyes. Many people, perhaps the young especially, find it a help not to use them much.

That's not to say that they haven't their own sensitive depth and seriousness. They certainly have; you have to be blind not to see it. However, it doesn't necessarily encourage the questioning mind.

They don't want to know what may be the name of the infinite sea to which we are all being swept on the swollen ever-rolling stream. Their concern is with the expression of their compassion and anxiety.

The nuclear disarmament issue, problems of ecology, of pollution and conservation, famine in distant lands, sudden disaster, the oppression of the poor in one tyrannical regime after another, the fate of political prisoners, animal welfare and vegetarianism – these and similar matters occupy them deeply. In this diverse concern the spirituality of our time seems to me to speak with imagination and genuine commitment.

And it's a spirituality of the people, not of their leaders. One of the remarkable features of our time is the inability of our leaders – politicians, trade-unionists, educationalists – to speak in terms of a spiritual ideal. They seem to be able to talk only in terms of money, jobs and success. The church is little better. All it can manage is some kind of appeal to us to get back to better days, to Victorian values or some other past point of moral achievement held to be praiseworthy compared with our current poor showing.

My list of the serious concerns of our time wouldn't impress everyone. To many people these various and apparently unrelated points of compassion and self-transcendence don't deserve to be seen as plotting the covert spirituality of our generation; but in my view they do, they are indications of important spiritual life.

It may well be the case that, as T. S. Eliot once said, most people live below the level of both belief and doubt, in the sense of below the level of conscious acceptance or rejection of Christian faith. They can, however, live what seems to me to be a spiritual life, and many do.

By people's 'spiritual life' I mean what they do to express either their sense of meaning and purpose in terms of some large view of life's significance, or simply their deepest concerns, in the sense of what they wish to identify themselves with and support when not swept off their feet by immediate self-regarding interests such as money, sex, prestige, emotional survival.

In such activity God is surely often experienced and loved and obeyed even if this fact is not acknowledged and verbalized, even if the word 'God' is never used for the inner drive and goal of these aspects of their lives.

There is certainly much more to a spiritual life than an acute sense of human suffering in certain places. A genuine response to God should be comprehensive, should include as much as possible of what life brings into our awareness, should persuade us to allow our commitment to God to function all the time. Earnest evangelists continually and mercilessly harangue us to reach such wholeheartedness; but who of us has made the progress necessary to bring from heaven that clear and wholesome light about our life?

One should thankfully acknowledge whatever light is in people's lives and not complain that it is not as bright as it should be. After all, some, perhaps many, Christians' devotion to Christ represents an investment of the self in what is a rather small fraction of reality. The last thing I want to do is to belittle the vision, the longing to be of the Son of Man's crowd, that is the good thing in their hearts; but I find it difficult to see why just because a life has at its base some kind of commitment to Jesus it is consequently entitled to the *cachet* of the word 'spiritual' exclusively.

I know an artist whose commitment to his art (and the tantalizing beauty always hovering over it, always near, rarely exactly there) is as total as any Desert Father's commitment to God, but for various reasons he hates the famous word I've just written and never uses it. However, what we all think it *means* is more generously clear to him than it is to me. He lives a spiritual life, if, as I believe, beauty is one of the many names which the Holy Spirit goes by in this mixed-up world. There is also failure in his life, and mistakenness and self-deception and indulgent hopelessness, and marvellous bits of courage, as in the life of all of us.

I see our time as a period of dominantly moral spirituality. Even in what used to be called its 'permissiveness' there is to be seen the characteristically English obsession with morality. What appears at first sight as 'anti-morality' is often just another kind of morality. It represents a life-style in which people are struggling to work out (though not necessarily with conscious purpose) important issues of freedom, honesty, personal identity, and also gestures of protest about a commercialized Western world whose values, or lack of them, some urge within them drives them to criticize.

The more overtly religious manifestations of this century –

evangelical piety, fundamentalism (whether of Christian, Islamic or Israeli style), and interest in techniques of contemplative prayer – form another side of the spirituality of today in which quite obviously the forces of progress and reaction are fighting it out.

It may seem that ours is very much an epoch in which ignorant armies clash by night, but it's not without flares over the battlefield in whose light some estimate of the forces for and against humanity is possible. The important thing is interest, to try to interpret and assess what's happening, instead of being impatient and furious with it all.

It's wonderful the way enthusiasm comes back and the tide of the spirit begins to flow again, when people reflect inquiringly, imaginatively on their time, not taking sides for the time being, not being judgmental about it yet, but simply wanting to understand it.

* * * * *

The opinion is often expressed that the majority of people don't spend much time with either belief or doubt, as far as life's large-scale meanings and hopes are concerned. It takes considerable mental work to believe anything at all and negotiate the implications and problems that pile up as a belief begins to take shape and command in one's life.

That is not a criticism, and it certainly doesn't mean that such people are not religious. They are indeed religious, but their religion is a thing of suggestion and silent request – a very pure and delicate thing, sometimes brutally manhandled by earnest servants of the Lord. Our wanting and thinking and feeling vary all the time, come from different levels of our being and hold different amounts of what we are. Occasionally a desire may come from so deep in us and involve so much of us that it will be religious language we want to use for this unexpected thing that has liberated us from life's literalness. It's a great help if you know a bit of the language and your mind can go a little further than just fumble for lost notions of transcendence. Many people can only fumble.

Then, too, faith is such a difficult thing to talk about.

Matthew Arnold spoke of the language of religion as 'poetic, literary and approximate' and how mistaken people are (both within and outside the churches) to think of it as dogmatic, literal and exact. Music, poetry, myth, suggestion, symbol, metaphor, silence – religion seems to be expressed more successfully through these than by most other means.

I wonder where you got the idea that there must be something wrong if you and your faith are on bad terms, as you say, and not speaking to each other much. That one's faith should every so often be disconcerting is a sign of its reality. It shows that you are not just playing around on the edge of the only territory where peace is to be found.

Religious faith is a mixture of privilege and burden. You can refuse this privileged burden so as to make things easier, but without it you are nothing in the world of faith, and in spite of all your praying and praising you have nothing to give anyone.

Baron von Hügel said once, 'Religion has never made me happy ... I have been in the desert ten years.' But he knew that that couldn't stand by itself and that the truth demands a rather less partial statement. One should remember he also said 'The final note of religion is joy.' Dr Johnson combined a vivid hold on Christianity with a fiendish disabling depression which, after its periodic attacks, left him just enough energy to fling himself on the mercy of his creator. Mme de Sévigné had an awful time because her beliefs were so settled and her emotions so unstirred. She couldn't understand why God had illuminated her mind but just could not unfreeze her heart towards him; and she often complained at having an enlightened mind but an icy heart, 'l'esprit éclairé et le coeur de glace'.

Throughout my ministry one of the points made by unbelieving friends that has most provoked me has been one form or another of the comment, 'It's all right for you; you're a believer. Lucky you. How good it must be to be able to believe. What a comfort.'

I have always wondered what on earth they could be

talking about. Certainly there are good things in the life of
faith, points of gratitude, of upholding, of interest, glimpses
of pattern in experience, and, above all, the mystery of Jesus.

But there is much else of a darker and more anxious
character, so much so that sometimes it's a question whether
the life of faith has done you any good at all or has just been a
waste of time played out to a second-rate hymn tune. And
then I think of those friends, and find myself saying, 'How
nice it must be not to believe. What a comfort to think that
nothing matters at the end of it all, not even my nagging,
irritating conscience.'

In this respect faith is no different from life. Life is much
richer and deeper than your experience and mine on a bad
day; and it is much darker and more menacing than happiness. I
imagine that the people who are most alive are the ones who
can bring these two together and live in the complex truth, in
an honesty that allows both the bad day and the good one to
speak and be heard.

*   *   *   *   *

It's not at all easy to show that religion does you any good.
Indeed the whole of the traditional propagandist attempt to
show that religious people are better, or in some way better
off, than so-called non-religious people seems to me a very
unsatisfactory procedure.

Religion may make you a happier person, and you could
well be better for that, but it may make you an anxious and
restricted person. It all depends on where and from whom
you learn religion and how you get caught up in it. Some
religion is escapist in exactly the same way that some atheism
and agnosticism are escapist – that's to say, it's a way of
ensuring that you don't ask the questions.

For people to live in this world unimpressed by its incomprehensible mystery, its danger, its beauty, never asking the
famous questions the painter Gaugin wrote under one of his
canvases – 'Who are we? Where have we come from? Where
are we going?', unwilling to look within and see whether at
the centre of their being is hope of some kind, and what – that

seems to me an unnatural way of going on, needing a lot of explanation.

Not that we know the answers to those three Gaugin questions, but looking for them is exciting. It's a help if, at a quite early stage of that looking, one realizes that God is not an object in a universe of objects, distinguishable from other objects, and identifiable by anyone who can rationally observe.

God is not a noun, the name of a person, place or thing. It is much better to use the word 'God' in a more relaxed way, as the focus of all that we understand as the meaning and purpose of our life, as the sum of all good, as the inner substance and value of each of the particular goods that so often shake our hearts with gratitude.

There are some quite common experiences that thinking people have always found particularly perplexing because they engage far more of our responding self than the situation seems to warrant; experiences of moral conviction, aesthetic enjoyment, depth of loving.

For many people these upheavals of the spirit don't require to be intellectually examined. It's sufficient simply to acknowledge that they are hugely important, are indeed what makes life worth going on with, and that it's wise not to let them go too easily by as though they are just ordinary. But there are also quite a lot of people who want to go some way into them, suspecting that there's more in them than meets the eye.

To some of these it seems that in these experiences the special engagement of so much of our being means that we are hearing the voice of the infinite, the holy, that many great and good (and indeed many wicked) people have thought is creatively and lovingly within our life and the life of the world.

This ultimate, it is said, invites, shames, excites, guides. We know we can't play around with it, but we want it. Christians believe that we are made to want it. It's possible that we are wanting it all the time, so that the adolescent wanting his girl, the careerist wanting promotion, the entirely secular wanting more money, the artist wanting more ability so that his vision can have its chance, the suicide wanting death, and so on (including so many of us who just want to be rather better people but our irritation with morality keeps getting in the way), are all wanting this ultimate that we call God. All these lesser wantings are each and every one fractions of a self that is made to want and to be satisfied when its wants are fully met.

The hunch of faith is that when the self operates not in fractions but as an integrated whole the truth comes out and it becomes clear that it is God that it wants.

As I've said, we don't know precisely what we mean when we use the word 'God'. Whatever it is, we can see it now only in a kind of blur, through a glass darkly (whatever St Paul meant by that exceedingly odd phrase). We shall know it clearly, we think, only by dying and being flung by that terminal blow into its arms.

It may be that all this kind of speculation is nonsense, and that this world is all there is, and that, however great our excitements, in them no window opens into a real beyond. I believe it to be sensible to be aware of this possibility and perhaps have scarifying arguments with ourselves about death and nothingness; but I can't see that anyone has put out a convincing case for settling for such a bleak view.

That's not to deny that some people do settle for it. That, however, is a choice of faith, a decision for a certain kind of faith, just as much as the religious interpretation of life is a decision for another kind of faith. And, like your faith and mine, the bleaker choice has to face the question why it should be considered to be so clearly the right stance before the infinitely varied and tumultuous experience that pours its incessant rain into human imaginations.

It's always a choice of faith. Sceptics and agnostics are as much believers in their own way as any other sort. You and I have chosen, pro tem, the religious interpretation of things, and so we are naturally deeply interested in others who have, who have gone further with it than we have, all whose perceptions (as Strachey said of Newman's) catch 'like a shower in the sunshine, the impalpable rainbow of the immaterial world'.

Religion is all one does to encourage one's appreciation of these spiritual experiences when they come and to make oneself sensitive and ready enough not to miss them. Jesus was very good, though sometimes terrifyingly so, on the idea of how much deepest life is commonly simply missed – by various preoccupations, angers, lazinesses.

I am sure we are right to think that God is there all the time, not only in our major experiences (love, beauty, tragedy) but in every experience. He is particularly, even if obscurely, there in life's mystifying injustice, its dreadfully boring ordinariness, and in the times when none of one's beliefs and hopes seem to fit and just lie in the mind like the fading leaves the wind has brought down on the lawn this autumn day where they seem scattered coins for which the departing summer has no further use.

\*    \*    \*    \*    \*

I don't see that the advanced age of many of the people in the churches should particularly create alarm, though it seems to bother you. Generally speaking, in recent years God appears to have moved to the suburbs, where he is much more widely admired than in the grey inner city or the rural depths. Congregations there are good and of varied age. Elsewhere, in England, what you say about the age of church people is largely true, and naturally so.

At a certain age most people realize that you can't go back, back to some peace or innocence behind all the losing and the mistakes, behind the waste of energy over superficialities and the swift retreat from the sudden moments of existential anxiety. And many of them are then ready to listen to a few of the ideas that have carried humanity's struggling thought about ultimate meanings.

Many such people have arranged the things they want from life in well-nigh final order and see that for them now the good that comes from reflection has a growing appeal. It's a

common view the world over that people in the second half of
life (to use Philip Larkin's words) will forever be surprising in
themselves a hunger to be more serious.

Whether this hunger is met by the fare offered in the
churches is another matter. I imagine that all of us in the
church would agree what an odd and difficult thing faith is.
To have it is to have within us a reality that is sometimes
radiant and worth everything we care to give for it, sometimes
extremely painful, and sometimes so silent it appears to be
quite dead. To it we struggle to adapt, from it we often
deviate, with results that are frequently ridiculous and sometimes tragic. It is not surprising that the church often dis-
appoints people.

Even so there's no point in plunging into pessimism. Most
pessimists are unobservant for quite a few hours of every day,
almost as unobservant as optimists. It seems to be an odd fact
of history that Christianity has always had a greater effect on
the world than Christians have themselves.

It's part of the mystery of the thing. There's no doubt at all
that what people like to call 'genuine' Christians, that's to say,
affectionate, altruistic, interesting men and women who
happen to carry Christ's flag, have been a positive and happy
influence in human life. Christianity's total effect for good,
however, has been primarily due to its continuing presence in
the world as a religion, as a way of understanding human life
and love, and as a liturgy – a historic imaginative and
emotional structure by which life is filled with Christian
meaning and we are enabled to hold the threads of experience
together.

And everyone who has had anything to do with maintain-
ing that presence has been important. Even those of us in the
church who have given the world baneful examples of what is
certainly not Christianity have incidentally helped to make
clear what the real thing is, because Christianity itself has
been continued, and these, though failing terribly to make
any sort of a go at living it, have all along been helping to
maintain the presence of that light that showed them up.

In just the same way, surely, the presence of Beethoven in the mind of the world is maintained not only by performers like Schnabel, Barenboim and Brendel, but also by millions of devotees, young and old, who murder the easy bits in the slow movements of the thirty-two sonatas on hideously out of tune pianos in front rooms all over the world.

All that matters is that the presence of Christ in the mind of the world stays. That presence is formed by the whole body of Christian saintliness and sin. Within that body is a mysterious source of life from which new spiritual ventures continually arise and fresh critical light is shed on everything, not least on religion itself.

Just now the church in this country is not particularly interesting, not one of the obvious life-enhancers that encourage and enlighten. To belong to it is to belong to a historic family that has come down in the world, to a household in distress. We have to hold to it till the life comes back into it and the blood begins to flow, and continually think and pray and argue about what in the will of God is the next step. Always and everywhere God wants something done or ended or started.

Faith is the positive conviction that one's existence has a meaning and the possibility of a final fulfilment. That meaning and fulfilment are what we are talking about when we talk of God and try to understand the gospel of Jesus. In the church that meaning and fulfilment are being discerned and acknowledged, lost sight of, contradicted, found again, by turns all over the place every day. The Christian life is a matter of exploring that state of affairs, living in it; it's a journey into the truth of Jesus.

*   *   *   *   *

As to your hang-up about evil and suffering and other sources of gloom: it's not difficult to make a lengthy list of the disadvantages of living in this sort of a world, nor one just as long of its good features. One is left with the old chess-board question, 'Is the world white with a lot of black squares on it, or black with a similar number of white ones?'

Which way one sees it depends to some extent on your experience, especially your early experience as a child and what brightened or darkened childhood for you, but also on your temperament, whether on balance you are a buoyant or a depressive type, and on several other matters of varying significance down to what sort of a day it is and whether or not you are in credit at the bank. I think that the conclusions to be drawn from giving life in general a good mark or a bad mark are almost as variable and unreliable. It's not a good line to take.

You ask whether our freewill could have been better programmed – for example, if God had created us able to perform only an infinite variety of kindly acts. I suppose one has to say 'yes, he could have made us so'. The result would have been (though it is quite unimaginable) a much less complex and interesting world, as indeed is the world of the simpler forms of organic matter where activity is determined by an inbuilt programme of automatic drives. In a world of human beings, able to act and react in a multitude of ways and to some extent free to decide in which way they will function, you will naturally have all the rich and terrible varieties of good and evil we know.

In a fine book called *The Foolishness of God*,[1] published several years ago, J. Austin Baker points out that in a painless world hatred, fear, jealousy, envy, cruelty, loneliness etc. would all have gone. However, in such a world no one would care; so you have to add to the list of what would have vanished in a painless world the tremendous items of concerned care and anxious love. That would be a vast amount to lose.

He also points out the unreality of this kind of speculation. We have never lived in a universe without pain. And to evaluate as superior a universe of which we have never had the slightest experience is a quite futile intellectual exercise. We can know good and evil only from the inside, from inside an

---

1. Darton, Longman and Todd 1970.

event and from inside ourselves. And if we ask the question, 'Is this universe the work of a good and wise God?', the answer can only be in terms of our own experience of it and what we think is good. Eventually we shall answer it according to whether, taking things all in all, we are glad that we have been born and given life in it.

I think that Western Christians have tended to be obsessed with the thought of suffering. Jews have suffered more than we have but they seem traditionally to complain in a less self-centred way than Christians, are kinder to God about it all, and achieve a kind of grave tolerance mixed with characteristic humour (there's very little humour in Christianity). The Jews seem to say to God all the time 'why have you done this to us?'; the Christian says 'why should this happen to me?'

Part of the trouble springs from the Christian habit of making so much of the cross and the crucifix. That image of death and pain, profound as it is, is inferior to the other principal set of images in the Christian imagination – images of life, growth, and new life.

It is not true that all pain is terrible. There is much pain in life that is a source of learning and insight. There is pain that is monitory, there is pain that plays an important part in the identification and appreciation of pleasure by contrast, there is pain that is part of the formation of the personality and the acquisition of various skills.

I realize that there is also a vast amount of pain that seems to be entirely negative and useless, an outrage to the rational mind. Some of the suffering the twentieth century has already had to endure is of a magnitude that no weeping, no compensation of demonstrable joys, can possibly wipe out. I groan as much as anyone about that, but I don't yet see much light on it all. I think the standard preaching of Christian truth in the churches, and the conventional arraigning of the universe on the part of unbelievers as well, are not particularly profound on the subject of pain.

\*     \*     \*     \*     \*

It's a great step forward in religious faith if one can find the asking of questions interesting and at the same time relax the

demand for clear answers or at any rate not be too disappointed when they don't come. It may well be that faith is
something whose depths are never plumbed by the clearest
explanations. Someone wrote in *The Listener* the other day of
being 'hounded by faith but hindered by theology'. He said,
'after one short conversation with a hot-gospelling word-
spinner I forget what faith is.'

A good deal of 'answering' goes on in the life of the church,
in the work of theologians, preachers and teachers. It is also a
common fact of experience that these answers tend to become
increasingly inadequate as your life of faith proceeds. It's not
that you think these good people are wrong and that you
yourself could produce better replies to what are after all
usually the most mind-storming questions people can ask. It's
just that you have an odd sense that you are being spoken to
in a foreign language or that what is being said to you is not
coming at you but going to the left or right of you all the
time.

What an excitement it is, what a relief, when you come
across someone whose speaking or writing about God comes
home to you and wakens your buried life, and existence as a
spiritual thing suddenly lifts up its head. D. H. Lawrence
once wrote that when reading new poetry he was like an
animal in a wood, pricking up its ears if it heard an unfamiliar
sound. If the sound turns out to be one of those of its
ordinary auditory world of everyday, the animal loses interest
and resumes its normal rounds.

That's also true of human beings, the believing or wanting-
to-believe animals going to and fro upon the earth. Most of
the sounds that come to us from the sacred wood of religion
are too familiar to rouse interest. It's the speaker or writer
that makes us prick up our ears who matters.

\*      \*      \*      \*      \*

The decay of the power of preaching is one of the great pains
in the life of the church just now. Affectionate and forbearing
church-goers who truly love their minister, both for himself
and for the Christ who in some mysterious, never adequately

defined, way haunts every ordained person, confess in moments of painful honesty that, while thanking God for the rest of their priest's work, as soon as he announces his text (or in some more radiant way signals the start of the sermon) they just have to switch off their minds if they are to keep sane.

We have to accept both what God gives and what he doesn't give. What is not given to us is as much a form of the presence of God as what he does give. I believe that firmly and truly with my mind, but I must admit that it's a belief that engages my heart much more readily after a decent meal.

For each generation there must be a kind of utterance that triggers off the mind's spiritual response and ignites the smoking flax of its desire for God. We don't seem to know it in our generation. It looks as if the Spirit hasn't given it to us.

Part of the trouble may be that it is a tradition that is speaking through so much Christian speech. The voice of the individual, the live person, the common or garden unsatisfactory mix of aspiration and failure that everyone amounts to, is hardly audible.

The voice of a tradition so easily becomes the voice of no one in particular to no one in particular. On the other hand, when someone with no axe to grind, no orthodoxy to defend, unexpectedly uses the word 'God' seriously, from some depth within, one looks up, one wants to listen. It's like the unexpected moments of excitement that come in a Raymond Chandler thriller. You are reading about a sleazy world of disgraceful people when suddenly there is some unexpected quick reference to Rembrandt's eyes, or the way the music of Mozart needs no comment and that's why Schnabel played him so much better than over-emphasizing Rubinstein did, or how much finer in this harsh world man's courage seems to be than his fate. A blind goes up, and beyond the mean aspects of these lives trapped in their corrupt concerns, you see another world altogether, of mystery and meaning.

The minister moves among us as someone hugely handicapped, like some old-time prisoner chained to a great iron ball, by the fact that people expect him to make noises about

God. He is the one who is there to do that thing. Even if he can overcome this by God-given talent to stir people's minds and hearts, no one can expect that talent to function twice or thrice a week. His hearers too have hang-ups and opacities that often make what they profoundly believe to be true sound just monumentally boring.

There are hints in the Bible that to be called to preach is to feel oneself to be the victim of a ridiculous mistake. Who, sir? Me, sir? You must be joking. We believe that God does in fact move in this mysterious way. He's at it more or less all the time.

So we should pray for those whom he calls. The responsibility is frightening, the world only too ready with its stockpile of guffaws and contempt; and the built-in temptations are legion, to elation, vanity, despair, the sick search for arresting utterance no matter what you are saying, the easy refuge of hiding behind the tradition lest those people out there see *you*, and the weary moralism, complete with the regular reference to Mother Teresa (fifty years ago the name of Albert Schweitzer had exactly the same role).

How ashamed one is of not praying for them enough. And for ourselves and our children; because Christian preaching is not a one-man show but a community-experience, made up of preacher, congregation, the communion of saints, and God. In this complex event the congregation has something to do without which nothing much can happen. About what they, the listeners, have to do we have been told very little. It may be something to do with being rather than doing, I mean, being in a certain kind of need, whose absence made even Jesus an ineffective figure in his home town and completely floored him in places like Capernaum.

That need may well be there in most people, but in many it is repressed in various ways – under defensive irritation with the spiritual, or a sort of personal modesty and embarrassment, or capitulation to the twentieth century view that, in order to keep going, trivialities will do if there are enough of them. And all the time there are thousands of people milling around life's busy ways, wanting to do something better with their lives than just live them. *Kyrie eleison, Christe eleison.*

I am sure that as congregations we would be helped if someone would teach us how to listen, what listening is when there is no obvious charisma to make the word of God a kind of seduction, how to make use of what seems to be this weekly realization that God is not at the moment doing much through sermons.

I know that in your work as a preacher you're always on the look-out for books. The two best books I know on the subject are an old one and a comparatively new one. The first is *The Ministry of the Word*[1] by R. E. C. Browne. The other is *The Way of the Preacher*[2] by Simon Tugwell OP.

1. SCM Press 1958.
2. Darton, Longman and Todd 1979.

# 2 *Forgiving*

Christians are committed to specializing in forgiving, though I don't suppose anyone would spend much time claiming that they are particularly good at it. Anyway, how would one set about estimating their performance?

Buoyant and extrovert temperaments seem to find forgiving easier than brooding types whose imaginations keep treading the road back to old injuries. Both types tend to interpret as injuries various experiences of misfortune, hurt pride, disappointed expectation, broken dream that collect in the emotional baggage of most of us. It's worth while looking long and hard at these mistaken interpretations and correcting them, getting the right name attached to your pain. A lot of emotional gas would be let out of our lives if we did this exercise regularly.

I don't know that it's any harder to forgive someone who has died than someone who's alive. You can't observe any change of heart he might manage; you can't tell him you've forgiven him if you get around to that. Both those helps, and they are certainly helps, are not coming your way. You are more or less on your own, except for God, the mysterious other, who is always mixed up in our struggles. So the work of forgiveness has to be done mostly by you yourself, and, what's more, inside *you*.

There's some advantage in realizing that. Actually I think that the main part of forgiveness is always a work of adjustment and thinking and emotional re-arrangement inside oneself even when the offender is there, close at hand, because

I believe that forgiveness is mainly doing something about aggression and retaliation. It's a matter of getting your aggression diverted from someone, or the thought of that person, so that in time your love can flow through and take its place.

That piece of work is bound to take time, may even take the rest of one's life, may never be completed in this life. It's a help to realize that forgiveness is a job of that magnitude, not just a single unpleasant chore like clearing up a mess. It's more a matter of living with a dark situation and deliberately feeding constructive thoughts into it, so that it begins to contribute to one's life rather than just remaining an enemy, the secret malevolent sharer who won't clear off.

You say you can't understand why the official Christian point of view is so critical of anger. Isn't it natural and right to be angry, say, about injustice, and to use that fury as energy for dealing with an evil situation?

'Dealing with it' needs a bit of unpacking. If it is to be a sane way of dealing with it, it will mean either using imagination and effort, maybe with others, to remove the evil, or coming to the conclusion that nothing can be done about it at present.

The injustice that's been eating your heart all this time is this second type, because it's way back in the past. You can't do anything to remove it now.

You are left, however, with a huge gloom of memory and a whole lot of unusable fury on your hands.

All of us have lots of this stuff around; and very uncomfortable it is. So we either hide it away inside us because we are ashamed of carrying around so much hate, or because (not being particularly self-assertive people) we genuinely find it almost impossible to believe that we in fact have inside us such antagonistic feelings about this person or that or life itself.

And that's no use, because what's denied wriggles out and shows itself in one way or another – say, in our tendency to criticize other people for *their* aggressivenesses and hates or in our joining in the hue and cry against one or more of the current conventional scapegoats. The world is throbbing with so much displaced animosity, so many people and things taking the rap really meant for quite other people and things, so many lines crossed, that someone somewhere must see the joke. It's a wonder that any loving at all manages to find its way through and get done.

Most of us want to live with ourselves more honestly, more genuinely than this. Looking within, we are conscious of the drabness there, how quickly life goes, how little we can show that was truly some effort at contributing and not just a taking. We want more from ourselves than we've got, or anyone else has got from us, so far. Jesus understood that mood. I think he must have unsettled and excited many such people with his swift inquisitive look, as if bringing into their world just a suggestion of – well, of what a relief it might be to leave the conventional set-up of their lives and its tendency to moodiness and join him in some scheme of his.

Back now to the hateful ghost in your life. What's the point of keeping it up and being furious with him forever, of living backwards all the time and raging at a memory? You certainly can't get any revenge that way.

And there's always the possibility that he may be taking the blame for other things that you dislike, even some things in yourself that you disapprove of but don't want to dig out and face just now. So that the situation is in part just another example of the crossed lines that foul up life constantly and complicate every issue.

Sometimes, when our fury at someone is chronic, it may be that there is not enough interest, certainly not enough enjoyment, in our lives, and that hating a memory does put a kind of meaning into life, even though it is an aggressive and destructive one.

I don't see that there's anything unusual in things being as complicated and involved as this. And life would be much less interesting if we hadn't to sort it all out and try to see the confused motives of loneliness and love that operate in our enjoyments and hostilities. You said in your letter that you've been 'having a bad time with God' recently, that most of the time 'he hasn't been around at all'. Well, fortunately and unfortunately, he's always around. Complications are among the clearest of the presenting signs of his nearness.

The times in which we feel most emotion and perplexity (love, rage, guilt, fear) are the situations where the kingdom of God is particularly, urgently, struggling to come through, where the bodiless word is waiting to become flesh. The pain is the pain of birth.

Some people find it easier to do God's will if they think of their loyalty to Christ, and see the difficult reconciling gesture as to be done 'for Christ's sake'. Not all find it a help. People want to be loved for themselves, rarely feel enough of that best of human warmth, and they are naturally suspicious and let down if it occurs to them that they are just a means to someone else's notching up points in sanctification.

The only way I can make use of the 'for Christ's sake' idea is to see it as a kind of shorthand for enlarging the meaning of the whole situation, for seeing the injury, the offender, my pain, all bathed in the light of what Jesus told us life is for, the coming of love in the life of the world.

In a personal hurt, the whole thing, my coping with my pain, my treatment of the person who has wronged me and also *his* struggle with what his act has done to *him*, his own desire for growth towards reasonable and enjoyable life, however conscious or hazy that desire is – all that together is an example of the huge thing Jesus talked about incessantly, the coming of the kingdom of God, the transformation of love from a thing of talk and dream into reality. It's not just a squalid scrap between me and someone I just can't bear.

Jesus is the mediator, the bringer of this so much larger view of experience. That's the kind of meaning I see in the 'for Christ's sake' idea. I don't like the phrase much, but I think the idea helps.

Our happinesses don't need all this thought and care, but our miseries – they must have as much life, as much meaning, put into them as we can, or else they will contract and close on us and grip our hearts to death.

No one has ever discovered much of what went on in Jesus's brain. Neither the commitment of the devout nor the expertise and relentless enquiry of the scholarly have taken them very far into those convictions with which he negotiated each rapid day. What is given us, after centuries of poring over texts and meanings, is a few glimpses of what may have been just the surface of his mind.

Underneath is a solitary Jesus no one has ever seen – the emotions that stirred him but didn't resolve in expression, the recurring images that made up his outlook most of the time. Every so often, however, he becomes clear. And his worry about anger the havoc-maker and his belief in forgiveness the reconciler are as clear as anything we have been told about him. Those passages in the New Testament which bring that Jesus before us will always make the most self-assured of us wonder whether we have looked long enough at life and felt deeply enough.

I don't think he ever thought that his ideas on these matters were exactly reasonable, in the sense of being likely to pay off. Someone has said that Christian love 'attains its true essence when no more accounts are kept'.

Sympathetic people have a good start when there's a forgiveness job to be done. I suspect that most of us give ourselves a higher mark for sympathy than we should. Having taken the point, it's quite right to go on to say that sympathy is not in conflict with the truth. The truth is that you have been treated very badly indeed. No one would blame you for thinking him a horrible bit of work.

Our moral judgments are part of the interpretation of life by which we make sense of it and save ourselves from floundering out of our depth. Sometimes they are just the shallow end of things where we can touch bottom and feel safe. If we once entertain the idea that something we thought wrong may in certain circumstances not be so, we feel insecure – there's water under our feet now. The greater the

insecurity the quicker is the imagination's retreat to judg-
mentalism and moral inflexibilities of one sort and another.
I'm simply suggesting that he may not be quite as bad as you
think.

We tend to assume that anyone who has done wrong could
have acted differently. It is sensible not to be absolutely sure.

I can't measure the lack of vitality that makes one person
submit to temptations which a more robust person would
resist. I can't know the power of the environmental forces in
his life that have been part of him since his earliest days. I can
judge facts; I cannot estimate a person's moral worth. I can
even, given the appropriate information, describe how and
why he seems to have developed certain regrettable character-
istics. But it's not in my power to say how guilty he is, or that
if he had tried he could have acted differently. I may think he
deserves nothing but pity, or I may feel that from the facts at
my disposal it does seem that if he had made a little extra
effort he could have avoided the wrong behaviour that stands
to his name. But I can't be sure of either.

All I can be sure about is that, being human, I don't know
the whole story. The only one who knows the whole story is
God. It follows that in the Christian view the only sort of
judging that is reasonable is simply the judging that is an
objective understanding of a person's behaviour; it can include observations on havoc caused and harm done, but all
estimates of moral worth and assessments of guilt have to be
left to God.

We have our work cut out to achieve this kind of objectivity.
Here are a few 'spiritual exercises' for the wounded. I have in
mind anyone who has been hurt, let down, wronged, and is
finding it difficult to get rid of the pain.

1. Accept the fact that this injury has happened to you. It is
as much part of a full life to be hurt every so often as it is to be
particularly pleased with things every so often.

2. Accept the fact that you resent it. There is no need to feel
guilty. You are not an exceptional sinner – simply someone
who has come into a quite common bit of human injustice

and unhappiness. Practically everyone has some reason for being furious with life.

3. Find out exactly why you resent this person, *all* the reasons why you are angry or just dislike him/her. Grade these reasons in importance as honestly as you can. The less important ones can be ignored. The work has to be done on the important ones.

4. Recognize that some of the resentment may refer to past experience, past injustice or deprivation, that cannot now be undone and must necessarily be lived with. To your dying day you will be a person who suffered that particular pain at that time.

5. Recall that some part of life's *goodness* you do have, and you do enjoy it. Some of this is absent from many other people's lives. Of them there will be those who long, enviously and maybe resentfully, for what you have and they have never had.

6. As for this person who has injured you – his or her defects of behaviour and personality have causes that go back a long way. Many people have had unfortunate experiences in childhood which they have never been able to cope with and absorb and neutralize. It's true of all of us that we are both victims and victimizers; we all live hurt as well as hurting lives. If you knew *all* that has hurt him (including the hurt he is now not aware of) you would find a good per centage of his unsatisfactoriness explained – not in the sense of being *excused* but in the sense that you would be in a position to *understand* a good deal of it. And you would probably want to be merciful.

7. Try to reduce indulgence in aggressive and vindictive thoughts. In the inner monologue that is part of our continuous, and not consistently distinguished, mental life, it is worth while trying to cut down the 'telling-off fantasies' that express our anger and to some extent do relieve us. We can find better forms of relief. There is enough anger in the world without us adding our bit. In all situations where forgiveness is needed, it's usually anger that blocks the reconciling spirit.

It's the anger that needs attention, not the injury. Nothing can be done now about the injury.

8. As a bit of long-term preventive spiritual health, it is good deliberately to increase the amount we think of things, experiences, people, that we *like*. The presence of appreciation is a fantastically important part of a healthy life. But it is rather vulnerable. It needs deliberate cultivation just as much as we need deliberately to get regular fresh air.

9. Pray for the person who has injured or disappointed you. The absence of warm feeling (probably impossible anyway) is nothing to worry about. Pray in a quite matter of fact way that he may come to know God's will for him, whatever it may be (you don't know it), and that he may be given grace to do it. The eucharist is a good time and place for this.

# 3 Men and Women. Security. Three Stages

People seem to find increasing interest in the myths of creation in the first chapters of Genesis. If we alone of all creation are made in the image of God, men and women are more like God than anything else in the universe. It must follow that to understand and love human beings is the best way of coming to know and love God. That's the nearest we can get to him in this world of time and space where all knowledge of God must be partial and indirect.

To seek God in himself is to follow a wrong track, and perhaps a risky one. The Bible hints at mysterious dangers in such a purpose; we would find that we couldn't look on that face and live. But hidden in people's lives, there he must surely be. When someone, rising early, draws the curtain, sees far off in the distance the day's appearing edge, and feels the night in his heart begin to lift and leave, or when two people after long conflict forgive one another at last and end the dreadful waste of years – there is God. So we think. And if he's not there, who cares where he is?

Then there's the infinitely touching way these early pages of the Bible announce how much men and women need each other. Incidentally, I see this myth not as a statement of some pre-mundane catastrophe but as a parable of human spiritual growth.

The dark voice said 'you shall be as God, knowing good and evil' (that's to say knowing everything). But when their eyes are opened, when they have this infinitely desirable thing called knowledge, all they know is that they are naked, that they want each other, need each other, are in themselves, as individuals, quite insufficient and very vulnerable. And it agitates them and makes them frightened and confused. 'We are not at all like God, knowing everything. All we know and see is that we need each other.'

To be exposed suddenly to tremendous truth is over-whelming. There is the need to cover and take cover; and the story tells of a covering and a hiding. When people go through some over-whelmingly self-revealing experience they often want to withdraw from life for a while, can't face any more of it just yet, must sort this lot out first.

A crab must shed its shell periodically, as it grows too large for it. After shedding its shell, it goes away and hides somewhere in the marine world until its shocked and tender body begins to acquire a new and more practical shell, and it can face life again.

Human beings, too, tend to hide when they're hurt or have come into some disconcerting revelation. Some people have been hurt so much, or so early, that they are now hiding most of the time – in some falsehood, dream, illusion, vanity, that seems to make life bearable.

When I said[1] that men and women have the same funda-mental need of security but that this need will be expressed by the sexes in different ways, I meant something like this.

I think that the feminine sense of security is always related at its root to biological function, that's to say, to some form of the nurturing role, in motherhood or career, and it doesn't matter which so long as its quality is rich enough for her to know that she is part of some meaningful purpose. It involves usually a satisfactory relationship with the community. And it is particularly well-founded when she knows that she is loved by someone.

On the other hand, I think that the masculine sense of

1. *The Following Plough*, Epworth Press 1978, p. 102.

security is very often related to a man's need of success in one or more of the countless forms success can take. The other side of that coin is of course the fear of being unsuccessful; and because of this fear a man has a tendency to confine his life to those areas of experience in which he feels more or less in control. Consequently, at any rate with Englishmen, his security often involves some clamping-down on emotion; and that is an impoverishment. Emotion is essential to a full life, though it carries the potentiality of taking you unawares with its overwhelming power. I think many men bury much of their gift, much of what they have to give, like the man in Jesus's story who hid his talent in the earth.

These are very loose generalizations, by no means new, but there's quite a lot of common experience to illustrate them and they have occurred to many people. Reports from the world of those who try to help in troubled marriages suggest that one of the most destructive forces in marriage is simply the failure of men to understand women and women to understand men. We do need to unpack the differential meanings in the words of the Bible 'male and female created he them'. And we do need to notice the varying part played by the need for security wherever two people love one another.

I suppose there must be some lovers who are fully satisfied in each other. Each is all the other wants in human relationship. No one can tell how many such lovers there are. They can't be the majority.

For the rest, a kind of drama of security is going on all the time. To the insecure person the devotion of the other is needed on a large scale. Their being together, as well as expressing their loving, has an additional function in allaying anxiety. The more insecure of the two will the more easily have panics of jealousy if signs appear that the other can, or needs to, love anyone else, even, sometimes, anything else.

Someone who has a rich mental, aesthetic, spiritual, socially well-orientated life, will consequently have a variety of sources of vital satisfaction and security. The love that such a person can actually *give* may well be richer but it will be less anxious, less demanding, and may seem less total than the love of one who has put all his or her emotional eggs into the one basket of human loving and wants the one relationship to carry the whole of life's importance.

Christ has divided many households in this way. Where one lover has a fuller life, and especially a life whose windows are open towards Jerusalem, it will inevitably be a life with, somewhere in its depths, a divine dissatisfaction that no earthly reality can meet. There will always be some whisper of doubt as to the quality of what tangible forms can offer. As Scott Fitzgerald wrote in *The Great Gatsby*, 'no amount of fire or freshness can challenge what a man can store up in his ghostly heart'.

I am grateful for the feminist movement, but I have the impression that it is concerned mainly with correcting the imbalance between women's and men's power in the social structure, and also, perhaps, in expressing a long pent-up feminine rebellion at historic masculine domination of life. However, what we really need is not a fight but more understanding of what it is to be male, what it is to be female.

Man cannot know who he is without the help of woman, without her telling him what she sees him to be, what comes over to her from the world of masculinity. And woman can't know who she is without the help of man, without man telling her what image is projected to him from her, and how his needs, conscious and unconscious, modify that image even before he receives and assimilates it.

All this can't be done without words, without verbally expressed mutuality and openness. Unfortunately ours is a generation distracted from that exciting prospect by the reductive efficiency of the telephone and the compulsive triviality of television.

In the beginning was the Word. The ultimate is a kind of saying. Not cleanliness, but men and women speaking to each other, heart to heart, is what is next to godliness. But in our *fin de siècle* epoch we are like the victims of a thrombosis, struck, paralysed, in that part of our being that deals with speech. We may well have to learn all over again how to talk.

*      *      *      *      *

Those who think that when two human beings love each other they are simply doing what comes naturally must be joking. Loving and being loved is a learning and a discovery.

All of us want love but we are not always able to recognize it. Pleasure is something we register quickly, but love is a more complex affair.

We may be quite unable to recognize it because of mistaken expectations or insatiable inner demands that are hangovers from the past. Life can say to someone 'Yes, look! You are loved, you have in your own life this tremendous thing about which so much beautiful and fatuous stuff has been said and sung.' Yet because of our immaturity, with its infantile ideas about love, or our woundedness, with its secret longing for a love that will compensate for some persisting sadness, we can't see it, for we don't want the real thing. We want an easier, more immediate, more obvious thing than love.

To love someone 'as oneself', as our Lord said, must mean to want the other to be his or her full free self, not just an 'as you desire me' satisfier of one's needs, not just a redeemer of one's past. It must mean to be delighted and hurt by love as lived out on the basis of that want, and to see that the delight and the pain are precisely evidence that you have in your own life the real thing that love is. There may be more of this real thing in your own situation than you realize just now.

Marriages have a natural tendency to become more 'spiritual' with time, even when neither lover is consciously turning to God. And by 'spiritual' there I mean a relationship that has become a deeper and more diverse bond, and more elusive, depending less on observable physical and incidental pleasures. Its substance of memory and gratitude and belonging and tension has accumulated as a deep deposit from lengthy experience of good and ill.

The two may well excite one another less and irritate one another more; and this is partly because they have become more aware of their differences as mature human beings. It is precisely their loving that has helped these differences to emerge, because it has given them confidence and freedom to evolve as selves. St Augustine said 'Love means – I want you to *be*.' It would be a huge mistake for them to regret the result of that want, to make emotional issues out of the emerging differences and think they are signs of the disintegration of their world of love. Underneath, unrealized maybe, the meaning of their being together is stronger than ever, like a great persisting tide under the turbulence that comes and goes above it.

As a matter of fact this can be true in an ironic way in a marriage that is not at all in good shape and actually doomed. So many years of your life may be tied up with someone you've come to dislike in a number of ways that nevertheless the long indulged-in thought of leaving him or her suddenly surprises you by its apparent logical impossibility. The poet Conrad Aiken must have been a formidably attractive and infuriating mate. After he had married for the third time, his second wife Clarissa, on being asked if she missed him, replied 'Of course. After ten years together I would have missed the Abominable Snowman.'

Under the surface there are unseen realities which have an enduring life and continue to plead their case.

I wonder if you know the work of the poet Thomas Blackburn. It is worth a lot of reading. Here is a poem of his called 'Gold Ring':[1]

> I do think a man and woman living together is
> commendable
> Though perhaps I only say so since it is the way I have
> chosen.
> But many of us find complete solitude unendurable.
> I both incline to agree with them and think it is a benison

---

1. First published in *The Tablet*.

If endured without too much strain, and it's that makes,
well, marriage possible.
You see after the party or the good bit of news
God, though no doubt an ideal one, is a somewhat remote
listener,
Whereas to be able to remark on a dress or happy event
To someone whose life we have decided to share
Confirms our being alive by an answer to the statement.
Moreover being a sexual creature, and promiscuity
Bringing such complexity invariably frightens off
communion,
Where is incommonness I affirm fidelity.
After all, though I know about the new faces, new
excitement et cetera
It's surprising what novelties there in fact are
And how one, common as breakfast, can be transfigured.
Of course, he or she or both may be intolerable
But Love is wise, and assuming a certain care in choosing,
It's probable that one cannot bear the other since one finds
oneself unbearable,
And that enduring a little more of another personality
Is not unlike – a better word – I say 'forgiveness'
Which more clearly is a condition of being able to see,
And of not caring too much about being trespassed against
or one's own trespass

       *        *        *        *        *

It has often occurred to me, when thinking about prayer, that
the traditional idea of three phases or ways of the spiritual life
(purgative, illuminative, unitive) has some echo in the life of
domestic love.

In the married life of two people who have had the patience
and the luck to get it all together and make it come good,
there can be traced an initial period, sometimes stormy, in
which their minds are released or purified (though it's a rotten
word for it) from ignorance and insensitiveness about what is
involved in living and loving at close quarters. They are now
led to see that their former lives as individuals are really very
poor models for their new life as a pair.

Then comes a phase of enlightenment as to what men and women are in themselves, in their masculinity and femininity, and how each reacts quite differently to being loved, disliked, ignored, trusted, made jealous, encouraged, and so on.

There is a third phase, of unity, in which the principal tensions and conflicts of the earlier phases are over and the two are one at quite a deep level, in a love that is a kind of 'ground-bass' to life. They are now confident enough to be open to the reality of other people, the world, and maybe God himself, who is said to be the fount and origin of all love.

These phases are not successive but interwoven, with episodic anticipations and regressions, which make existence the complicated thing it always is. It would be a mistake in time of trouble to assume that you are far less united than you actually are.

In a marriage that lasts many years two people learn a huge amount about each other, continually moving towards and away from each other in the alternations of attraction and antipathy. And as this swing of experience between good and defect keeps going on it's impossible to work out the account to a balance. They just know they have grown together, that they belong – they have become more or less one mixed thing, almost one composite person, unimaginable when they first married. Through the years they have been again and again delighted at being together, and often disappointed by the renewed realization that in various ways their needs and interests are quite distinct. Jesus, who had such a keen sense of crisis, such a sharp perception of the element of reckoning in life, also saw how often the opposite is the case, how there are situations in which reckoning is out of the question and people must let things be for the time being, let life's mixture grow together just now.

Love and unease grow together in every marriage, and in the end the flower of it all draws its attraction from that double root. The reasons for staying together in a grown marriage are obviously quite different from those for getting married.

One bright thought that should come in the purgative phase, and does so if you're lucky, is the uselessness of perfectionism and the way it drags monumental miseries around human life. No one is ever going to make anything of loving who believes that ideal happiness with an ideally satisfactory partner is a human possibility.

There are many people who miss a lot in this world not because of misfortune, nor through laziness, but through a kind of indolence of which they are scarcely aware. They are secretly waiting for life to yield some perfect thing they believe to be hidden in its folds for them.

This continually lessens the amount of themselves they can give to the present. There is no sacrament of the present moment for them. The present moment, however good, is at best a kind of hors d'oeuvres. The main dish, the real thing, will come before long. They are, as J. B. Priestley said of the characters in Scott Fitzgerald's novels, all creatures of longing, all 'wanting better bread than can be made out of wheat', and so forever hungry.

*　*　*　*　*

I've been think about those parents and the son with problems. It's good, when you are in some crisis and trouble of growing up, if people can see some way into what is happening within you (you can never actually tell them) and sympathize and have faith and try to encourage. This can't mean anything else than that they love you, truly love you in your struggling self, and are not just interested in your behaviour and correcting it because it frightens them.

To be overly concerned with a person's behaviour is to be already on the side of what's hurting him. But to see the person himself and what he's fighting for, hoping for, is the sort of spiritual love that brings life, enables him to live, enables what is coming to life in him with such difficulty actually to emerge. For all of us there is no better school for learning what love is and how to do it than wanting to know better someone who needs love rather critically. One of the first lessons in that school is to see the mistake in thinking that you will convince people that they are wrong by showing them that you are right, even when you are.

# 4 Candlemas and Beyond

It's 2 February; and I wish our churches took more notice of Candlemas, such an attractive day in the Christian calendar. Jesus's parents were understood to have taken their six-weeks old baby to the temple for a customary rite of devout family life. Christians later began to see layer upon layer of meaning in the scene as St Luke's Gospel imagines what happened when Jerusalem, the city of promises, received the promised saviour (2.22–40).

It is not officialdom that greets him but an old man and woman who have been waiting through the disappointment of the years until all that's left of their hope is a little surviving courage. Then the old man is seen with Jesus in his arms, marvellously happy because he now has the truth that makes a religious meaning of life. He hasn't much more time, but that doesn't matter. He will die a happy man because making sense of life must necessarily mean making sense of death.

So in many churches at Candlemas they carry lit candles round the church and sing *Nunc dimittis*. They could be saying, among other things, that through Jesus the light of 'my Father's house' has been shed over death, and everyone whose eyes are bright with its reflexion can depart in peace.

That is possible even though the world's secrets and concealments are yet to be unmasked, even though it is still true that there can be no love without cost, without a blade in the heart.

We find what meaning we can in experience. What is so 'adult' and intelligent in believing that the scepticism of our time is right and that all religions are a tissue of illusions? That is to insult the innumerable pilgrims of the spirit who sought in one imperfect way or another the ultimate meaning and love which they felt must be hidden away in it all.

I realize that we are not doing this all the time, this serious seeking. Much of the time we live trivially, boringly, or in satisfied immediacy, or in disgrace. But in the large experiences our minds, maybe unwillingly, are forced to think and ask.

Whenever life goes deeper than usual we become aware of this pilgrim self in us. The you that wants to find some answer to your death-questions is the pilgrim soul that's in all of us. It's as worth while a part of our being as any.

More is given to it, more perceived by it, than our superficial self realizes.

I think John Welsey had a sense of the reality of hell that you and I would hardly share, but there is evidence that what he recoiled from most was the thought of meaninglessness. In a letter he wrote to his brother Charles in 1766 he said, 'If I have any fear, it is not of falling into hell but of falling into nothing.' He is a man of all times in such a remark, not just of the eighteenth century.

If our Christian understanding of God and life's purpose is more or less on the right lines, it must surely include the thought of continuing life after death for us, the complex creatures he has called into being.

About the prospect before us there are plenty of people who say 'Of course there's nothing.' Among such friends it's possible to feel slightly inferior for believing otherwise. You needn't feel inferior. They know absolutely nothing that you don't know. Their denial is often little more than the left-over of adolescent rebellion against traditional orthodoxies, but of course not always so – there are some good arguments for there being 'nothing'.

However, no one, but no one, knows anything at all about what happens or does not happen after death. All that anyone *knows* is what we all know – the huge pain, the mourning, the questions, the protests, the rage 'against the dying of the light', all the classic gloom about death – and the bits of light that flash in it like stars, the serenity here and there, the courage, the faith that has enabled many people to go through all that death is.

In all this it seems that religion is sometimes a support and sometimes pretty useless. There is nothing anyone *knows*; and anyone who says he knows what's what about it, even if he's got an odd sort of collar round his neck, is really a bit of a nuisance, contributing little to the subject. And the conventional sceptic is a nuisance of exactly the same size.

We have to use our wits, sifting out what is probably illusion or projection, and evaluating what remains, especially this thing that refuses to be jettisoned, this deep surmise that things don't end in death, and the possibility that this surmise might be a kind of seeing.

*       *       *       *       *

I know that you like trying to get your thoughts down on paper. Later on, when your feelings begin to settle, if you can find the time and the mood, it might help if you wrote down some account of the experience and the shifts and changes of feeling it has caused.

It will help, at least, to put some distance between you and all you've been through. That could make it more manageable. By making it something you are thinking about, rather than an upheaval that's throwing *you* about, the writing could prepare the way for your seeing some kind of meaning in it or at any rate some kind of hope in it.

Dr Johnson was once writing to a friend on the loss of his mother and he suggested that he put down on paper as much as he could of the experience, and of his brighter memories of her. He added that this would be a comfort to him later 'when your grief will have matured to veneration'.

Some people are able to digest experience through thinking, objectifying, contemplating, while others are constitutionally not able to do it that way but must do it through action. I think that perhaps men are made in the latter mould more than women.

One aspect of bereavement seems to be more severe than it used to be, and that is its loneliness. People seem to be unwilling to come into your pain, don't want to hear you talking about what you're going through, who you've lost, what it's like to be left. Their nervousness and embarrassment may spring from fear. People are as frightened of death and all it can involve in pain and perplexity as ever they were, but in the fading of religious belief about it they have now no words for any of it. It seems better not to try thinking about it.

If this is in fact the case they will be nervous about people talking about their grief because that brings this forbidden subject too near them. It touches their fear and exposes their not having any thoughts and hopes about this great dark matter or their having had no encouragement and help to think and hope about it. They may even think they are helping you when they change the subject and won't let you talk.

That could be sometimes unconscious rationalization, and what's really happening is that they are helping themselves though they don't realize it.

Many bereaved people want to talk because this means being restored to the human community after their solitary walk through life's shadow side. It's good if they can be helped and encouraged back. If friends and acquaintances can't rise to this, what then? Well, we have to learn how to love and also how to go without the love others are unable to give us. This will be the pattern all the way through until the broken kingdoms of this world, with their happiness and their bewildered silence, become the kingdom of our God and of his Christ.

✻   ✻   ✻   ✻   ✻

I don't think our generation can take seriously the thought of what in an earlier time was called 'preparation for death'. In any case, it can't be a special exercise. It must be simply going on with what one has been trying to do all the time – that's to say, living the life of faith and trusting that in this way the spiritual self, the self that loves and likes, admires and appreciates, sympathizes and trusts, will mature, or at any rate grow and so be ready to be raised to, or born again into the life beyond death, to continue its growth in that incomprehensible dimension.

A hugely important part of the life of faith, which Christian instruction has not been very successful in teaching, is learning how to accept time, and time's continual habit of taking things from us and in various ways shifting the scenery.

In the broadest sense this is learning how to mourn, learning how to love and let go. It's never too early to make a start on that, even in youth, though people who have a shallow view of youth don't believe you need to start so early.

There is a fine poem by John Berryman[1] called 'The Ball Poem' in which he observes a small boy playing with a ball at some water's edge and losing it as it bounces into the harbour. He sees this as the boy's introduction to 'responsibility in a world of possession', to learning

> The epistemology of loss, how to stand up
> Knowing what every man must one day know
> And most know many days, how to stand up.

One of those who had learned the epistemology of loss was Dr Johnson. One night (it was the herald of the end here for him) he woke up to find that he had had a stroke and was partly paralysed and unable to speak. First of all he prayed to God 'that however he might afflict my body he would spare my understanding'. Then, to see whether God had in fact done that, he wrote some Latin verse. He later admitted that the lines were not very good but from the fact that he realized at the time they were not very good 'I concluded myself to be unimpaired in my faculties'. That sort of sanity and serenity and engaging good humour spells out how fine human beings can be.

1. John Berryman, *Selected Poems*, Faber 1977, p.16.

To read the Gospels is to be much cheered by Jesus's intriguing combination of faith and a seemingly boundless scepticism about current religion. And then, all through his teaching, there is his continual, clearly happy, suggestion that while God is far from us he is also amazingly near.

It does seem that it had never occurred to him that life could be some awful downward slide. He wasn't attacked by that kind of gloom.

He was, however, keenly aware of the havoc of anxiety. He warned us against unnecessary anticipations. If the right preparation for death is to learn how to live this life as fully and enjoyably as possible, it looks as if 'and live this day as if thy last' is rather a melancholy way of putting it. Sufficient unto the day is the evil thereof – and the goodness too. The evil has to be borne and dealt with as far as possible; but the good has really to be enjoyed and savoured with unreluctant delight. You won't get the full taste of the goodness of a meal if you use as a condiment the thought that you may never have another.

It has all to do with flexible response to change and loss all the way through, and at the same time enjoying things to the full. It's impossible to express this without giving the impression that one doesn't really enjoy to the full but has acquired a rather precious skill at distancing oneself from experience and can see beauty, love, achievement, youth, vanish without being particularly perturbed. No one wants that.

Truly to love and enjoy must mean to be vulnerable. I am sure that human beings are normally responsive beings and that those who don't seem to love and enjoy much are in that unfortunate isolation from life because for some reason they are afraid of being hurt or have already been hurt more than they can bear.

It may well be that if you are able to 'kiss the joy as it flies' you will live in 'eternity's sunrise' – but who can do that good thing without being so far above it all as to be living in the next world rather than this? A good part of the fullness of life is, as one of our hymns says, 'learning all the worth of pain'.

Oddly enough, I've never found the Christian idea 'even so in Christ shall all be made alive' much use in helping the bereaved, though it seems to me to be absolutely central to the Christian hope according to the New Testament. I think it doesn't penetrate their sadness because it is just too theological and complicated and provokes too many questions (eg. who exactly is 'in Christ', how do you know whether or not you are in that fortunate condition?). All this makes the idea too difficult to have much bearing on the heavily emotional business of death.

I find some of the simpler comments on death quite stirring and communicative. In one of Milan Kundera's novels he makes much of the German saying *Einmal ist Keinmal*, what happens only once might as well not have happened at all. Don't you think there's something in that? If we have only one life to live we might as well not have lived at all.

And Henry James, that marvellous man, about whom Max Beerbohm said that as a moral authority he stood out as clearly as any preacher he'd seen perched in a pulpit, said similarly in a letter to a friend 'It takes one whole life for some persons, *dont je suis*, to learn how to live at all; which is absurd if there is not to be another in which to apply the lessons.'

Words and explanations take us only a small part of the way in trying to form even the vaguest wish about something so absolutely unimaginable as resurrection. Yet for so long in the human story there has been this longing for resumed or renewed existence in some other world, under other appearances and meanings, with other routes to joy, at least until all that we question is explained and all that's unfinished is completed.

I know that you can refer all that to the instinct of self-preservation and say that it is just life, unwilling to surrender itself to the dark (even though it knows that every bright day drops into the night), trying to make our intellectual being its ally.

Another view, however, is possible. The inner force of that

unwillingness, struggling so ineffectually for what it thinks could be the truth, is in fact the Holy Spirit within us struggling to bear witness to our sheer intellectual inability, and pleading that we are not as smart as we think we are when we limit life to this ambiguous mundane affair, and that, on the contrary, we are children of God and can go forward, trusting him for all that's to come.

*　*　*　*　*

You asked for some idea about how to pray for a suicide. Is this any use? I'm afraid it's in the Thou-form which may not be the preferred style for you. I found I just had to use it. With the thought of one of life's bitterest riddles in my head there seemed to me something perverse in addressing God as someone I knew rather well.

> Almighty God, Father of all, have mercy on those who in their darkness and despair have taken their own lives. Grant to them new life in thy love, new understanding and hope. Forgive us for whatever part we have had in the wrongness of things that made life unbearable for them. If it be in thy purpose, grant them blessing from whatever faith and love the Spirit works in us here and now, and some part in thy aid to us as we here seek to do thy will. So may the ties that bind us all in good and ill remain and hold unto everlasting life.

*　*　*　*　*

I am sending a few thoughts on your worry as to whether God will separate you and your husband in the next world – you having had faith to rely on and work at all the way through, he having never had any interest in religion.

We know very little about what faith is exactly, and so about what the absence of faith is. It is certainly a *kind* of faith, and a fine kind, that shares the life of the church and is able to stand with friends there and say the Creed with a willing heart. Your husband wasn't exceptional in not being able to do that. He wasn't alone in finding formal Christianity uncongenial. Many, many people are in the same situation, particularly men, and more particularly, English men.

But he had some hope for himself and his world, some idea of what he could consider good, just, compassionate, and so on, was often amazed at the high colour of sunlight at a day's ending. And, I hope this doesn't sound too pious, if we could imagine him being questioned about it, we know that on the way to Golgotha he would sooner have been able to give a hand to the man struggling with his cross than stand with the ignorant rabble shouting at him.

We believe that anyone who wants to be guided by what he can see of justice and mercy is doing the will of God, even if he doesn't use such language. And we're convinced that in matters of rightness and goodness God does not want us to say or do any more than we can genuinely, honestly say or do. We are so accustomed to the idea that God is no respecter of persons that we tend to forget that he is also the supreme respecter of persons. He doesn't pressurize.

As for your husband's criticisms of what means so much to you and me (incidentally, I used to think he was often very amusing and perceptive – there's so much in religion to give everyone the creeps), you have to remember that a person's apparent rejection of faith is something just as slippery and uncertain as apparent faith. I rather care for some of the thoughts in the New Catechism of Christian Doctrine that Father McCabe has produced for Birmingham. To the question 'Have all atheists rejected the gift of faith?' the answer given is, 'Not all who are called atheists have necessarily rejected the gift of faith; they may merely reject some particular image or understanding of the mystery of God. In such matters, only God himself can know our hearts with any certainty.'

And I much admire the intercession in the Roman Mass in which prayer for the dead is expressed like this: 'Remember those who have died in the peace of Christ ...' and goes on, simply and comprehensively, ' ... and all the dead whose faith is known to you alone.' Often, when I read that, my heart heaves with a rush of gratitude at the thought of nothing escaping God. Even if there's only one minute bit of what he wants in a life, he'll see it, he'll not lose it in the bleak disintegration that's ahead for us. And all the unfulfilled promise that still awaits its hour – he won't let go his hold on that either.

How he makes these deep assessments is another mystery. People who get irritated and want it clear cannot have it clear, and they may well make things much darker for all of us, indeed have often done exactly that in the past. One just holds to the thought of the wholeness and continuity of life, of a resonance of meaning between our mixed affairs here and the life beyond, and looking unto Jesus gets on with living for today and in today.

I agree that there are some frightening things in the New Testament; but there are also indications that the judging business is God's, not ours, that we are completely out of our depth when making ultimate or even provisional spiritual estimates of anyone, including ourselves. I interpret Jesus's comments on the last being first and the first last in this way. What he's talking about is the outrageousness of calculation, of doing shoddy moral sums – who's right, who's wrong, who's saved, who's unsaved – who on earth knows? Just wait and see. There shall not be left one stone upon another that shall not be thrown down.

To make a lot of the uncertain and mixed character of things doesn't make life casual and superficial. It makes it livable. It gives the lie to pessimism. It encourages the deeper and longer look. For example, we live in a society that seems to think there are only two important things in human life, success and failure. I don't criticize it for that, only for the thin meaning it gives the words, and for not seeing that, as far as success and failure go, each can be hidden in the other, and probably is so in every life. There must be many surprises, and much forgiveness, when all is revealed.

As to the thought of separation in the life to come, it may help to think a bit about just how important relationship is to us.

In ourselves we're nothing much, indeed hardly anything at

all. There's nothing there to transcend death, be resurrected, or whatever, or hardly anything. This is why the ancient Greeks, and to some extent old Israel too, could only imagine life after death as a shadowy drift of wraiths and ghosts. They didn't see that relationship is really of the essence of us as human beings.

We don't really exist in ourselves. Unlike the flowers in the garden I see from this window that open and fall each in its solitary world of silence and evanescence, for us it's the case that relationship and communion make us what we are. By ourselves we actually find it difficult to bear ourselves, long to be close enough to maybe just one human being to share whatever joy or catastrophe comes. We owe our very existence to other human beings, we need others for our continued growth, we come to our richest fulfilments in association with more and more human beings, in pleasure and suffering, in trust and obligation. It looks as if life is for, was made for communion, an infinite inter-relation of giving and receiving.

There are many people to whom this thought has come so vividly that they've gone on to sense that life and death, this world and the world to come, are in reality one tremendous eternal whole. Some New Testament sympathy for this way of thinking can be found in St John's Gospel, especially the idea that when we live most deeply and affectionately this wholeness of life becomes clearer and even palpable.

I'm sure its best to think of heaven in this way, not chronologically but axiologically, in terms of that depth of living now in which we are already in to it, rather than in temporal terms, as some future realm of judgment and reward.

God made us this way and for this. That's why it seems absurd that we should be thrown on to the scrapheap of death just when these great realizations begin to dawn on us, as they do when the lights of youth begin to flicker. I'm not thinking just of the resurrection of the individual, because, as I've just said, we're almost nothing in ourselves, and any life after death must involve the relationships in which we most realized our personal being.

It was in the providence of God that you and your husband lived for over forty years, sharing this, unable to share that, quite often sensing that depth of things in which hints of the eternal wholeness come – all of which adds up to learning what love is and how it's done.

I came across an intriguing remark the other day, attributed to an obscure fourth-century martyr. 'God *cannot* do what is disgraceful, and he *will not* do what is ridiculous.' I'm not trying to console you. Our power to console is not particularly robust; but we do have a strong sense of the ridiculous.

And it seems ridiculous for God to begin with two people this complex business of learning what love is and not go on with it just because death has appeared on the scene. If life is not to be obviously ridiculous, what he has joined together he will not put asunder, as though in some childish rage that death has broken in and spoiled his work and made it pointless to go on with it.

There must be other, and we imagine more creative, opportunities for us all to go on with the purpose of being who we are. What those opportunities will be it's impossible to say. I realize that strictly speaking we cannot make a single meaningful statement about the life beyond death. There are no words for what is unknown.

But what is in fact quite definitely known is the predicament and mystery of beng human and mortal. Human beings will never stop wanting to talk about that, never get rid of the inner compulsion to confront it and struggle to find words, or words plus sounds (Mahler's Second Symphony), or just sounds (Beethoven's Last Quartets), for what's exciting and troubling their minds when they do confront it.

My faith and hope are that after death we shall go on with learning how to love God with all our heart and our neighbour as ourselves, because Jesus made it clear that doing that is the purpose of our being created at all. That must mean that the personal relationships in which we have most learned, and learned most of, what we do know of love, will go on, to become richer and fuller, to be added to and extended, until we come to that fullness of life which is too wonderful to be siezed and held in thought, but can be, will be, thoroughly lived in love.

# CONSIDERING PRAYER

# 1 Private Prayer, Repetition, Children and Prayer

There must be a price to pay for the presence of so much noise in the daily life of our time. It's not easy to identify the damage it does to us exactly. It must have something to do with the need for silence that has asserted itself in spiritual life today.

People know that their lives are too cluttered, they dream of solitude and quietness and space; but they usually do nothing about it, either through inertia or they may even feel vaguely guilty about wanting to put a bit of distance between themselves and our twentieth century that's so throbbing with work to be done. At the back of their minds, however, biding its time, the thought persists that some day they'll have a go.

And in your letter you say you are thinking of trying whatever good going on a retreat will do for you.

There is so much interest nowadays that there are many different kinds of retreat. In the traditional silent retreat of three days the conductor develops some theme, relating to our desire for God, in the addresses he gives in the chapel (usually twice a day) and is also available for conversation about one's life of faith if requested. The rest of the time is all yours for prayer, reading, relaxation, rest, and whatever worship the house normally arranges. There are such things as individual retreats under the guidance of a spiritual director, for eight days or even a month. These are advanced and expensive affairs that I haven't yet tried but they look as if they really do take one's mind and soul to the cleaners. There are private retreats, group or parish retreats, in a religious community or retreat house, with a great variety of programmes, very different from the traditional sort, but carefully arranged for retreatants of different types and ages, of different religious experience or none.

You can obtain information from The National Retreat Centre, 24 South Audley Street, London W1Y 5DL. The Centre issues an annual journal, *The Vision*, which gives details of all retreat houses in the country and their current programmes.

The traditional silent retreat is more helpful if it is held at a convent or monastic community where there is the full tradition of daily worship in the chapel. The alternation throughout the day between the solitude of one's room and the community of worship in the chapel puts a wonderful rhythm and a quite fresh perception of time into what you are doing.

The silence may seeem strange at first, and being such an unfamiliar void it can even agitate one a bit. I think that our endless chatter may relate to an unconscious fear that if we let silence exist and do its stuff it may leave room for some sharp memory, some unsuspected quandary. Indeed it may. So some patience is needed. There's no point in attempting to evaluate a retreat until it's over and you are back at home.

It can be seen as a short programme of training, consisting of silence, prayer, worship and rest, in an unfamiliar but specialized atmosphere. The first time may be a bit of a test, in the sense that it's a bit of a test coping with an unfamiliar routine, putting up with oneself at close quarters without the opportunity of getting away from oneself – but that's all part of the idea. For centuries it has proved a surprisingly good formula for sharpening the spiritual appetite and enlarging one's spiritual experience. One of the great plagues of the spiritual life is boredom. We need variety of spiritual stimulus if we are to keep at it. A retreat is a useful bit of quite dramatic difference put into the few things one does to satisfy the desire for God and bring a clearer and more wholesome light about one's life.

The silence is not just the external thing; it has to do with the need for silence within. That particlar need must have been in human beings for ages, an odd, persistent affair, always mixed with a kind of fear.

Travellers and explorers have often spoken or written about the mixture of fascination and fear in the huge silences they have known – in the desert, at the summit of mountains, in the vast, tense calm of the night at sea under the heavens, the work of God's fingers. Yet they always want more of it, or to go back to it. There is a kind of call in just the memory of it.

Most of us don't have this deep experience. We are, however, all aware of the continual inner monologue of the mind, with its endless liking, resenting, wanting, fearing, and how good it is when for this reason or that it quietens down and lets you realize that you are not just a disorganized human being but a person, wanting a clearer idea of why you're here and some vision of where the grace of God may conceivably be.

And that's only the beginning of it. People discover a certainty of the rightness of being still within, and at the same time the usefulness of it. What ought to be done, or what it would be wise to do, in this or that perplexing situation, often becomes clear to those who will drop their problem for a while and be still and just know that they want God.

The great contemplatives have been willing to let the silence flow around that greatest of all names too, for a while giving up the attempt to say in a patter of syllables and meanings what we think that one famous word signifies. They have been content simply to direct their longing towards the cloud of unknowing that seems always to hang between the rational mind and God. There is infinite good to be found in this strange exercise.

\*　　\*　　\*　　\*　　\*

There are many people for whom it is practically impossible ever to be absolutely alone. There are many for whom it is extremely difficult to find ten minutes of silence in any day. The amount of private praying of the traditional style that you can do without solitude and silence is far more limited than is usually acknowledged.

On the whole priests and ministers have taught a programme for people's spiritual life that has been either too burdensome or too dull. It has stemmed ultimately from the monastic world. In that world programmes of prayer, worship and spiritual reading are part of an organized daily life. They cannot possibly be norms for twentieth-century men and women living 'in the world'.

It must be a mistake to think of the spiritual life, what we do to express our desire for God and deepen its importance, as something that is done or goes on in such time as is left after our life at work, in the family, in social and recreational activity, is over, or in such time as we can deliberately make by pushing out some of all that. For better or worse all that is in fact our life.

The monastic life is essentially the result of responding to a call literally to come out of all that and live an altogether different kind of daily life, one that is deliberately and with historic skill arranged to give prayer a major place. What the monk renounces is pretty well what constitutes life for most of us, the rational enjoyment of possessions, sexual love, parenthood, the use of power. It is a mistake to think that lay people, to be properly Christian, are called to do a mini-mini-version of what the monk does. Yet much traditional teaching about prayer seems to indicate the presence of that assumption.

I'm not saying that it's easy to answer the question 'then what can I do, or must I do?' I wouldn't want to use the word 'must' at all. New patterns have obviously to be worked out, and they must be worked out with ordinary people rather than prescribed for them. Lay people must say what helps them to love life and people and endure what has to be endured, and what keeps the image of Christ in the mind, what drives it away, what brings it back. From a lot of talk of this kind we shall find new forms, infinitely various forms.

Meanwhile, I think highly of the work of the late John Main OSB[1] in his efforts, remarkably successful as they have been, to teach ordinary people a form of contemplation. And always one turns gratefully to the sort of attitude that figures so frequently in John Chapman's Spiritual Letters. For example, in Letter XII:[2]

> As to advice, I can only tell you what I think. I recommend you prayer, because it is good for everybody, and our Lord tells us to pray. As to method, do what you want to do, and what suits you. It seems obvious that most spiritual reading and meditation fails to help you, and the simplest kind of prayer is the best. So use that ... but one will not get any satisfaction out of it, in the sense of feeling 'I am good at prayer,' 'I have an infallible method.' That would be disastrous ... Nor ought one to expect 'a sense of the reality of the supernatural' of which you speak. And one should wish for no prayer except precisely the prayer that God gives us – probably very distracted and unsatisfactory in every way. On the other hand, the only way to pray is to pray; and the way to pray well is to pray much. If one has no time for this, then one must at least pray regularly. But the less one prays, the worse it goes. And if circumstances do not permit even regularity, then one must put up with the fact that when one does try to pray, one can't pray – and our prayer will probably consist of telling this to God.
>
> As to beginning afresh, or where you left off, I don't think you have any choice. You simply have to begin wherever you find yourself. Make any acts you want to make and feel you ought to make; but do not force yourself into *feelings* of any kind.

* * * * *

1. See, for example, *Word into Silence*, Darton, Longman and Todd 1980.
2. *The Spiritual Letters of Dom John Chapman OSB*, Sheed and Ward 1944, p. 52.

Not many of our people seem to have been introduced to the thought that many actions can rightly be regarded as prayer if done with a spiritual desire or intention. It is a releasing and enlarging thought and one to make prayer much more interesting than it normally is.

Curiously enough, prayers memorized for repetition have a significant place in the process.

I think that those who have traditionally suspected repetition in prayer (particularly those brought up in a Free Church tradition) are beginning to shake free from this inhibition. It was derived from several factors in their experience – a misunderstanding of our Lord's criticism of 'vain repetitions', a basically Protestant wish to be free of the mechanistic structure of late mediaeval Catholicism, and a failure to see how much sterile repetition had in fact developed in their own tradition.

The ideal of extempore prayer is as historically conditioned as everything else. The great days of Free Church extempore prayer belong to a time when vital and gracious speech was much more common than it is now. That kind of speaking was not only a characteristic of public worship. It spread into domestic piety. I recall the days of my childhood in a ministerial home. My father left school at fourteen years of age and thereafter had to educate himself. And this, as so many of his generation, he seriously did. His command of the English language was fed on the systematic reading of three authors – Shakespeare, Dickens and J. H. Newman. I recall him wearing out by much handling three copies of Shakespeare. Consequently, when he prayed in our family prayers after breakfast, the language and the thought were things which we as adolescents couldn't help respecting. What eventually got us down was this particular act of domestic piety in itself; and when he saw that we had in our individual development grown away from it, he sensitively abandoned it. But we have never forgotten the weight of meaning in his language of address to God on behalf of the family, nor indeed the elegance of the English our parents used in their weekly letters to us away at school.

It seems to me that all that has vanished. Public prayer in the Free Church traditions, where it is still extempore, is as mediocre and predictable and unmemorable as it is in the revised liturgies of the more formal traditions. So it is now more than ever important to have by heart some of the deep and beautiful prayers of the past that say it so well and incidentally contain so much Christian memory.

The work of people like John Main and the widespread growth of interest in *The Way of a Pilgrim* and the 'Jesus Prayer' have provided a new atmosphere of acceptance of the value of repetition.

Another help is to make use of your knowledge of another language if you have it. In the eucharist, when I return from the altar to my place, with whatever that solemnity has planted in my heart, for many years now I have been peculiarly satisfied in saying two prayers in Latin (a language I love) – the *Anima Christi* and then, after an interval of silence and suspension of any kind of thought, the *Salve Regina*. I have done it for years, and I love it, and I find myself quite disappointed, when I am among the last communicants, if the celebrant doesn't allow a period of silence and stillness at the conclusion of the rite to give us all time to do what we want to do.

*   *   *   *   *

Children's prayer is a very special subject on which you need the comments of a specialist. I'm not one of those. A lot of work has been done in the last fifty years on what religious ideas a child can absorb and use, and the findings have been critical of much traditional church teaching.

On the other hand there has also been extensive study of the relation between the imagination, the understanding and the unconscious. This has produced other lines of thought – for example, the realization that the value of words is not confined to their being understood, and this in any age group.

Generally speaking I would want a child of eight or nine years of age to be taught that God wants us to live a happy life and that he helps us to do this, especially the more thankful we are for this and that and the more we love people. Christianity is about thankfulness and loving.

Loving is of course very different from liking. Loving means understanding, appreciating, thinking generously, and responding to people's needs.

A child needs to begin learning a bit of this as soon as possible, especially what loving can be done when you don't like people; but I don't think much of it can be grasped before the age of eight. Certainly I don't think a child of four can be (for example) kind, to a brother or sister, when not in the mood, and such a child oughtn't to be made to feel guilty when unable to manage the kind gesture.

Back to your boy of eight. I would want him to begin to learn the rudiments of honesty with oneself, so that he will be less likely to be overwhelmed when he is angry with life and furious with people, and (without instruction) to be given a few ploys that help to dissolve anger.

I think he should be taught the Lord's Prayer, given some introduction to its meaning – at any rate enough for him never even to dream of asking God for any material thing. I would try to get him to learn one or two of the more intelligible, and in any case beautiful, short prayers used by adults (preferably from the liturgy), and I would tell him several times that millions of people have found that it is good to be silent for a while with nothing, not even the thought of God, in one's head.

Whether he could make anything of it or not, I would want him to start hearing that prayer and the sacraments are the most interesting things in religion, and that, for the rest, being religious is a matter of enjoying as much as possible of all there is to be enjoyed, and joining with other people in helping things to come right for those for whom they are pretty awful.

It's good if he can begin to see what an interesting person Jesus was and why so many people have thought it a sensible thing to regard him as very special indeed. Sooner or later, and it must vary a lot from child to child, he must be helped to see what a miracle is, and what it is wise to ask God for when we pray for other people.

Now I have written this, it all seems to me rather a load of stuff. If it is anywhere near correct, it must all be done with a very light touch. I think a child should be saved from 'getting religion'. I have seen just a few religious children. They have given me the shudders, seeming in a peculiar way malformed.

Sin is something that I would not mention until he brought up the subject.

# 2 Intercession

There's your paragraph about being unable to see the point in the church going on relentlessly bringing to God's notice matters like Northern Ireland, the Lebanon, famine in Africa, and so on, about which he is presumably rather better informed than we are.

It's not in order to inform God that we include such tragedy in our prayers. We can't inform God about anything. Some Christians believe that God knows about every pain before it has reached its victim, and somehow sees now what you and I have yet to suffer. That's a thought to make one quite nervous.

Whatever the truth about that, we pray about such matters first of all to express our distress and anxiety. Prayer has always had this meaning, among others, of being a way of expressing the Christian's feelings. It is as natural for believers to express their distress, horror, bewilderment to God as it is to express their love and gratitude.

There's more than that to it. In any act of intercession, quite a lot of religious life is involved that extends far beyond the moment of saying the prayer.

We bring our concern (e.g. Northern Ireland) into all that we believe about God's purpose and his way of working in the world. Most of this attempt to see the issue in the light of faith is done in meditation outside the actual prayer that completes it. This may result in a new appreciation of something God wants us to do ourselves, but we believe it certainly does help us to be more ready for his will both as regards this particular issue and generally.

As to the actual praying, rather than the meditating, there are a number of teachers nowadays who see intercessory prayer as simply a matter of being with God, in the presence of God, with so and so (whatever it is) on one's heart. It is not so much a matter of asking for favours for someone from a supposed omnipotence but part of the desire for God's presence, a form of realizing it in association with the particular need that is at the moment our concern. These teachers consequently see intercession more as a kind of the prayer that is usually called contemplation. There is some help on this in chapter seven of Michael Ramsey's *Be Still and Know*.[1]

To pray for others does also lift from our experience of life's pain and problem the depression, the fear and hopelessness, that so easily descend on us when we think of such aspects of the human condition without religious faith.

I think that the depressing character of so much of the news in the media every day is responsible for much of the obscure undercurrent of unhappiness in many people's lives. They have so little long-term hope and trust, so few glimpses of meaning, to help them interpret the failure and the fear in things and make possible some replenishment of their dream that life may yet one day come good.

I'm not saying that faith automatically comes up with cheerful explanations, but I'm sure that faith grows and deepens as we try to understand and endure for Christ's sake. The grimness of life either pushes you into unexplored areas of your faith and gives you a bigger thing than you thought you had or else it dries you up inside and leaves you with nothing.

The praying for others that's part of one's private praying is best kept within one's personal experience, concerned with people one knows and loves and with people one often meets

1. Collins Fount 1982.

at work or elsewhere. I see no point whatever in individuals in their solitude repeating the wide-ranging prayer of the liturgy. Private prayer and the liturgy are meant to be two different, and complementary, kinds of offering to God.

How God weaves our prayers into his purpose is something we can hardly know here and now. We believe that he wants us, wants us here and now to do what we think is his will, and wants us to help others do it. It is part of his purpose and providence that our faith and love shall help them. In this kind of faith Jesus himself prayed for his friends.

We have Jesus's assurance that God is intimately involved in all that we do, and in all that happens to us, whether to momentous or scarcely noticeable effect. His purpose takes into account (this was Jesus's way of putting it) even a falling sparrow's final thud on the road.

Nothing falls 'without your Father'. All that falls does so within his love. And all must mean all – from the plane losing height through a fog to crash into a mountainside to the petal drifting through a summer afternoon to meet its ascending reflection in a garden pool. And when the eschatological dawn lights up the faces of the blessed, every creature will be seen to have been given an essential and unique place in God's infinitely various caring, in a totality of good that will have drawn into its fulfilment all the love and disaster and sin that have ever been.

St Paul said, rather enigmatically, that since all we've ever truly wanted from God, and thought promised by God, receives a resounding 'yes!' in the faith of Jesus, we can consequently in the faith of Jesus respond with a resounding 'Amen!'

It can't always be resounding. Sometimes our Amen can be said, if sincerity allows it to be said at all, only from what Dostoevsky called 'the crucible of doubt'. But sometimes one can say it with such meaning and gratitude that once won't do, and one thinks of the Amen sung again and again, with florid arabesques of sound, by a Welsh choir at the end of an emotional hymn – to show that Amen means Amen means Amen.

My defence of this way of thinking, which could well be thought extravagant, is in terms of the famous three at the end of 1 Corinthians 13, the three realities that are going to be revealed as eternal, like three huge timeless rocks exposed by the receding tide of the sea of time. We live in hope, we live in what loving life leads us to think, we live in the faith of Jesus, who spent so much of his time gazing outwards towards things you and I can't see.

# 3 Devotional Reading

A teacher in an American theological seminary said recently
that devotional literature is a disaster area in church life today.
He spoke of its being either 'a wasteland of the tenuous and
the fatuous' or just presenting a writer defending some
particular 'ideological corner'.

I expect the opinion comes from one who has high
standards, and it's admirable to have high standards.

However, in what's called 'spiritual reading' one has to
remember that it's not true that only the best is worth
attention. Actually, it's not all that easy to define the best.

There's a sense in which the best must be whatever helps
one to hold on to a religious meaning appropriate to one's age
and need, relates significantly to what one is going through
just now, and encourages one to take the next step in God's
shadowy will.

That would be an existential, personal best. It could
be some writing that will never make the anthologies,
nor even a footnote in the next multi-volume history of
Christian spirituality. It could be a book or passage that
will never again seem to you particularly inspired; but on
one occasion it spoke to you in a way that stirred real feeling
and touched some part of you that was very much alive at
that time and needing to hear a sympathetic voice for a
change.

There are some books that last. Each one of us will select
differently of course, but none of us will have many. From
the huge pile of spiritual books that, out of duty, or historical

interest, or desperate hunger, I've read, just a few call me back, one or two quite often.

I would give all the writings of St John of the Cross and St Teresa, in one noble parcel together, for St Augustine's *Confessions*, the *Cloud of Unknowing*, and de Caussade's *Abandonment to Divine Providence*, and consider that I had vastly profited by the exchange. St John of the Cross (apart from his significance as one of the greatest of Spain's poets) and St Teresa are no doubt the preferred authors of the aficionados of speculative mysticism but little use to the Christian on the Clapham omnibus. I wish someone would get down to presenting imaginatively interpretative introductions and selections that would bring these two great names to life for the many.

Publishers of religious books seem to be in quite a good mood these days, at any rate as regards books of spiritual reading. They may not be laughing all the way to the bank but they are certainly not heading gloomily for the canal. The public for books of meditations, of selected paragraphs from the saints, of traditional evangelical piety, is large and could be growing.

With so much for sale, you just have to shop around, sampling this and that, until you come across someone whose way of thinking about God makes you read closer. We have to be honest with ourselves and not pretend to like what we don't like because we think we ought to like it, and we have to respect the material and give any selected devotional aid a fair trial.

It's good also to allow for the effects of personal change. If we don't change it's obvious we just haven't lived. The battering of experience inevitably dints and bends us; and we can be made restless simply by the passage of time with its continual unravelling of old certainties. And so it often seems that material that served us once, even inspired us for a while, has unaccountably worn out, and we have to look round again. All this could be one of the ways in which the Spirit leads and pushes us a bit further into the riches and the reproach of Christ.

Devotional literature need not consist only of what are usually thought of as holy books. Many of these are pietistic, humourless, perfectionist, addressed to the will rather than the imagination, and likely to leave you feeling peculiarly guilty or just rather tired.

What matters is whether the real you is being reached or not. Accordingly, it won't be material that informs or instructs you that you'll come to depend on but something that sharpens or re-awakens your desire for God, your sense of life's excitement and mystery, and removes the unpleasant suspicion that you are groping on alone. This writer has been where I've been. Many novels and much poetry have done this trick for me. Both are powerful forms of truth-telling.

I recently read, in a writer much involved in trying to work out a Franciscan style of faith, this comment on the line in St Francis' Canticle praising water and fire:

> When my soul is parched, reading the lines of a psalm, or a chapter in a novel by Willa Cather, or a poem by John Berryman, is water, and I am refreshed. Such reading for me is *lectio divina* ... In all the arts, sculpture, music, painting, philosophy, the fire, the divine fire, lights up the night ... in the twentieth century we have achieved the right to read the poets and novelists as part of our spiritual grounding.[1]

Because this kind of literature is primarily not instructive, because it appeals to something in us that's deeper than curiosity or the desire to improve our performance as Christians, it's important that it's read slowly and frequently re-read. The language must therefore bear the test of being read slowly and often. To be able to write like that is a gift from God.

For example, if I may mention my tradition, all are agreed about John Wesley's immense importance in the religious and social life of his country, his fascination as a man of God and a

---

1. Cornelia Jessey, *The Prayer of Cosa*, Winston Press 1985, p. 51.

personality, yet in the monumental and extraordinarily various amount that he wrote there is hardly more than one or two paragraphs that one would want to read twice, except his translations of German hymns (an important exception). On the other hand, his brother Charles, a man of much slighter stature, in his hymn that begins 'O Thou who camest from above' produced something that bears a lifetime's brooding. It should be learned by heart by anyone who wants to have always within reach a healing, refreshing, recalling statement of the essential Christian desire.

One of the reasons why religious books are in such demand today is that in our time there has been such a decline in the power of the spoken word in the worship and teaching of the church. All are dismayed about this. And there's a special danger in it in that it tends to drive Christians in on themselves so that they settle for a do-it-yourself spirituality.

The Christian life is much too hard for that. All of us need various forms of face to face contact with some other seeker. One of our hymns has the line 'He bids us build each other up'. There are many forms of that, and no substitute for it. Whether the other is a priest or lay person doesn't seem to matter as long as he or she is as interested as you are and as long as there is a genuine sharing of perplexity and question and discovery as we make our journey in Christ.

The number of people who are bookish in their religion is much smaller than we usually think. Many people are not helped by books at all, they must take some other route, they have in fact to do something. In Laurie Lee's eloquent prose elegy on the disaster at Aberfan, I like his story of the pubkeeper (the terrible landslide came to a halt just outside his door) who afterwards, whenever the full horror of the tragedy came over him again, would put on a tape of Handel's *Messiah* and turn up the volume high, ignoring customers' complaints. 'I always play that when I'm angry,' he said. 'I haven't time to read bloody books.'

The spiritual life of many people seems to go on quite a long way away from the world of books. There are things they hope for, regret, are thankful for, want still, and they know that it's all to do with God, yet when they fumble around in their minds for words to say something about it they just find emptiness.

If one is not bookishly religious, the fact has to be accepted – and absolutely without the slightest suspicion of inferiority. Twentieth-century Christianity is just too literary by half. It's worth remembering that for most of the history of the Christian church the vast majority of its members couldn't read.

There are other means of looking after one's faith and attending to spiritual needs. Much use has to be made of a mixture of memorized prayer and silent waiting upon God, and particularly of developing the habit of associating important experience with the thought of God – I mean one's major enjoyments and major miseries. Some Christian traditions give believers many things they can *do* in expression of their faith and their longing for faith. There is much to be learned from them.

# 4 Marian Devotion

I am glad to have the chance of adding to the answer I tried to give to the retreat group the other day when asked to explain my odd devotional habits, and particularly my interest in Marian devotion.

The Bible view of the creation of man is that he was made 'in the image of God'. That must mean that he is in some sense and to some degree like God, and so some kind of a picture of God.

That must be true of all who have been created until now, male and female, in whatever situation of loving or only partly loving they were each, in their incalculable millions, conceived, and in whatever situations of being together or in conflict or in bitter isolation they have lived, to make the vast unimaginably complex continuum of human history.

All of them count, every single one of them, and indeed every one that is yet to come into being in the unknown centuries ahead. All of them are to be seen as necessary to make up that image, to make clear that picture of God himself who for some reason wishes to be known.

And of them all Christians single out one, Jesus Christ, as the one in whom we believe it is supremely announced to us that God's intention in creation and history is a *loving* intention, an unimaginably vast saving of us all from death, so that we shall be brought at length to the bright morning that is himself.

If we believe that about him, what a stupendous person he is!

And if we believe that about him, we shall begin to think how much therefore depended on his mother. We shall want to explore and interpret her special part in Jesus's being able to give us the profound truth about God he did in fact give us.

Several students of human nature have suggested that the initial relationship between child and mother in the womb is the physical (though of course not the only) source of both the human longing for an ideal harmony of selfhood and experience and the human dream of some golden infancy and lost paradise.

That mysterious desire and vague reminiscence have inspired poets like Wordsworth and others to write lines that stir our emotions so powerfully that we are really quite mystified; and we wonder what can be the meaning of the happy-sad turmoil going on within us, sometimes almost to tears.

That's just one significance to be sensed in the mother-child dimension. There's a lot more.

You might like to have a look at a very interesting book called *Home is Where We Start From* by D. W. Winnicott, perhaps the greatest English psychoanalyst, whose written work is now receiving admiring attention throughout the world.

It's actually a good book to read after reading Wordsworth's ode on the 'Intimations of Immortality from Recollections of Early Childhood'. It makes much of the fact that there is a profound sense in which the male is the secondary sex. Where we start from is a mother and child together, created by God to nourish each other.

As long as that relationship is maintained and developed satisfactorily and long enough, the cared-for individual will acquire a sense of being a real person, with the confidence to go into life with a forward-looking enthusiasm. 'Every man or woman who is sane, every man or woman who has the feeling of being a person in the world and for whom the world means something, every happy person, is in infinite debt to a woman.'[1]

1. D. W. Winnicott, *Home is Where We Start From*, Penguin 1986, p. 125.

For various reasons men have found it difficult to acknowledge this. Incidentally, though I love the Genesis myth about
woman being made from man in his dreamy sleep, made from
his rib, taken out of man, and think it full of intriguing
suggestion, I also see it as a form of unconscious masculine
protest, as the masculine attempt to assert a male priority.

The fact is that every single one of us, men just as much as
women, began life in the providence of God dependent on a
woman. As Winnicott says, somehow any evasion of this fact
or hostility to it 'has to be transformed into a kind of
gratitude if full maturity of the personality is to be reached'.

Many centuries ago this was in principle understood and
accepted with primitive reverence, and then gradually obscured
and forgotten. In our time it has been given to people like
Henry Moore, with his continually repeated sculptures of
reclining or recumbent woman, to recall to twentieth-century
consciousness the deep truth that woman is the place (in some
sense like the earth itself) where each one of us grew from
seed, and that, generally speaking, in spite of what she didn't
know and the helps that may have been denied her, she
carried, fed, and nourished us, and provided that multifarious
introduction to the very mixed weather of life from which we
became able to meet whatever was to help or hinder us.

I began to wonder why all this part of God's truth, the
complex significance of the feminine and the maternal, sounds
so feebly in the Christian religion. It was certainly absent
from the version of it in which I grew up. I came to notice its
absence, and feel the pain of that, more or less simultaneously
with the realization of the astonishing range of meaning in the
figure of the mother of Jesus if what we believe about him is
true.

There is very important evidence in the New Testament,
especially in St John's Gospel. I have tried to describe this
importance in my book *Friday Afternoon*.[1]

___

1. Epworth Press 1976, pp. 53ff., 87ff.

So I naturally turned to Catholic devotion, where, it seemed to me, this world of thought and feeling had its principal recognition in the Western church.

Not that I think the Roman Catholic Church has yet expressed this dimension of faith anywhere near adequately. In some ways it seems to have actually prevented the adequate expression and exploration of it by encouraging what seems to me to be immature and often sentimental Marian devotionalism and popular cultism. Under these, masculine myopia can persist, unchallenged, forever.

Nevertheless, I find myself responding to G. K. Chesterton's realization that the presence of the Blessed Virgin Mary is a kind of hallmark of the catholic love of the Redeemer throughout Western and Eastern Christendom, as contrasted with what claims to be Christian and indeed what aggressively claims to be non-Christian devotion to him.

In the Magnificat, the Angelus, the Salve Regina, the Rosary, there is a variety of meaning and use and a potent depth of appeal that keep stirring one's gratitude. Sometimes I think that, apart from the eucharist, the Angelus is just about the most perfect act of prayer that Christians have managed to make.

# 5 Ikon

You asked for some more thoughts about the Rublev ikon to which I referred in *The Following Plough*.[1] Try to get a short pamphlet by Basil Minchin called *Praying With Ikons*. It's interesting and certainly helps one to set about the sort of praying it recommends; and if you get a copy I am sure you will read it more than once.[2]

Ikons are religious paintings characteristic of the Eastern Orthodox Church. In recent years Western believers, both Roman Catholic and Protestant, have become strangely drawn to them; and many people in the West seem to be finding it helpful to have a print of an ikon in their homes as a visual aid to faith, a reminder of the eternal as the day slips by and the haunting questions obstinately remain.

As focal points for silent prayer they have no exact equivalent in the Western Church. Perhaps the nearest is the place which the Host in the Tabernacle has as a focus of prayer in Roman Catholic churches, or the Blessed Sacrament in a hanging pyx in some Anglican churches, but ikons are quite different as concentrations of meaning and a special power clings to them for those who are used to them.

They are not just paintings; they are products of prayer and

1. Epworth Press 1978, p. 78.
2. Julian Shrine Publications, Norwich 1979. More general information about ikons can be found in Timothy Ware, *The Orthodox Church*, Penguin 1963 and the relevant chapter in a fascinating and beautiful travel book about Greece by Patrick Leigh Fermor called *Mani*, John Murray 1958.

deliberately intended as a means of renewing the image of Christ in the believer's heart. They are sometimes carried in procession. Strange things have been known to happen then – healings, reconciliations, sudden honesties. In happy moments, in times of danger or suffering, when dying, a Russian Orthodox believer, it is said, will want to see an ikon, touch it, kiss it, be comforted by it.

Even so, the Orthodox don't identify the divine reality with the representation in the ikon, whether it is of God or Christ or the Blessed Virgin or an angel. And the paintings themselves almost suggest the mistake of doing that. The stylized scenes, the emblematic rather than human forms of the persons, the enigmatic and distant look on their faces, quizzical or world-weary (one's not sure which), all seem to warn the imagination against coming too close. They tell us, as the tumbling waves of the sea told St Augustine, not to settle for what our eyes rest on but to look further, to look beyond this paint and wood for what our desiring heart is seeking.

Yet there is in fact an intensity of presence. Orthodox believers think that the fellowship of love and praise that Christ and the saints have with the whole church is deepened by being focussed in the ikons and the prayers of those who gaze on them; and it just is the case that many people, and not only religious people, sense that a heightened reality seems to have gathered about an ikon that has been much loved and has stimulated so much faith.

When you look at Rublev's 'Trinity' ikon, even if only a print or a photograph of it, you are looking at an arrangement of lines, shapes, colours, signs, suggestions, that has had religious meaning for millions of people who all wanted God as you and I want him – and with our kind of mind, shifting unnervingly as it does between confidence and despair. We are not alone. Whatever is happening to any one of us in the *una sancta* just now is in some sense known, understood, shared throughout. It's wise to hang on to that thought when you're down. Without it you could throw up the whole thing for a quite small reason.

In the Rublev ikon the three angelic figures are said to symbolise the Father, the Son and the Holy Spirit, though there is I understand a traditional disapproval of a too precise identifying which is which of the green, the purple and the diaphanous blue. They are meant to suggest, not represent. They certainly suggest three persons sitting at mysterious ease in some hushed, very private belonging.

In Genesis chapter 18 there is a story of three strangers who are said to have visited Abraham in the grove of Mamre and received hospitality. In some other ikons of this theme Abraham and his wife are also shown, actually serving the strangers; and there are utensils and food. The strangers were duly fed by Abraham and Sarah; and there followed a solemn confirmation of the covenant between God and Abraham.

That confirmation was eventually marked by the birth of Isaac as the fulfilment of God's promise. That's to say, the whole incident (which is not without some amusing detail) was a divine visitation.

In the ikon the three angelic strangers have come to represent the Trinity for generations of orthodox believers. The table is transformed into an altar, with the chalice of the eucharist on it. There is a suggestion of a church in the background, and of the oak tree of Mamre, and of the majesty of God since the rods in the angelic hands suggest authority and office.

The thing communicates a remarkable silence. The angelic wings are touching, as though the three are bound together in some infinite exchange, of love maybe. To be in heaven is to be admitted absolutely into the world of love. In the eucharist, and perhaps in all deep love and reminiscence, it is possible to imagine an anticipation of that happiness; but that is a wonderful idea that I can never get my mind round while actually at a celebration, only in relaxed reflection some other time some other place.

Don't you think that's true in all sorts of ways? You need quiet and a bit of mental distance between yourself and your experience to give its meaning for you a chance to come through. People who have led still and reflective lives often sense what's going on, what's coming, what could come, before others who may actually be much cleverer but live more temporally, more at the phenomenal speed of things.

Abraham gave hospitality to three strangers in whose shape the Bible understands God appeared to him at the oak of Mamre. He welcomed them, though he hadn't a clue about their intentions or whether to be pleased or afraid.

That is the way experience comes most of the time – out of the blue, often not meaning anything at first, just a knock on the door. We open the door, and we find that we are asked for some service; or it's pushed open unexpectedly and what we see on the threshold frightens us. But in the story the three strangers were much more than friend or foe, they were really God, coming to confirm his promise that Abraham would have a future of fulfilment and dignity. It was a promise so unbelievable that his wife split her sides laughing. 'Ridiculous!' she said; 'you know very well how it is with us. You know what we are wanting, you and I. A chance would be a fine thing!'

If we hear too often the inner voice of our sadness (whatever its cause) we don't notice the pile-up of negative expectation within us, and the inability to think that what's coming to us could be good, could be God, will indeed be God. All we know is that occasionally a breath of sorrow ruffles our peace and we stop what we're doing and stare into space.

Abraham welcomed the strangers. A later generation called them 'angels', but the Bible doesn't. In the Bible the three men for whom Sarah and Abraham cooked lunch were three men, and there is no suggestion in the story that they looked or were any different from three ordinary travellers. Afterwards, much later than the book of Genesis, they were called 'angels' because they were recognized as bringing a message from God. If God was discovered or realized to have been in an event, then the human agents or interpreters of it were seen as angels.

The word 'angel' means a messenger, one who brings you a meaning. Angels are not extra-terrestrial beings but ways of giving imaginative form to certain ideas, particularly the conviction that everything that happens is packed with spiritual opportunity, has God in it somewhere, showing the way, offering some grace. One just can't see this every time, and it's ludicrous to feel spiritually inadequate and guilty about that; but it's worth recalling, and often, that a good part of happiness is the dignity and radiance given to life by spiritual meaning, by significance that comes from faith in the presence of God in this, that, and the other thing.

These angelic beings in Rublev's ikon, who were originally three strangers in Abraham's life, have been deeply reflected on by millions of believers since. And many of them have thought how each day life comes, knocks on the door, bringing sometimes good and sometimes ill, and how the ability to welcome it, at any rate open the door to it, receive it in whatever shape it comes, and do something with it, is very much to be desired.

Everything comes associated in one way or another with God the Father, God the Son, and God the Holy Spirit; it comes with God actually in it, wanting something done and giving the love in which that thing can be done. I believe that, but I so often find myself believing it not with all my heart. I believe it with all my head, but I want more than that. I want to believe it more consciously, emotionally, and with trust – that is to say, with all my heart. And that's one sort of prayer that's prayable before Rublev's ikon.

# 6 Eucharist

For a long time there has been some critical doubt about the words, in I Corinthians 11.24, 'Do this in remembrance of me.' In my view, whether our Lord did in fact or did not ask his disciples to repeat the taking of bread and wine in memory of him is a problem not worth working at for long. The complete verification of any recorded moment of the past is hardly possible anyway, however much midnight oil you burn.

A saying of Jesus, a crime some innocent man is charged with, or just what you said or did with whom last Tuesday – these, like all events in time, are matters that immediately begin to blur and disintegrate as the present in which they occur is sucked back into whatever diminishing reality the past has.

Practically all that we live by, and would hope to be given the readiness to die for, is of faith. Christians believed from the beginning that Jesus wished to be remembered, recalled, in this way. They acted on this belief. And so began very soon a sacrament that is now loaded with centuries of accumulated re-calling in all the experiences of need or grace in which believers have found themselves as they struggled to come to terms with life's mystery and the inescapable image of Jesus.

The hold of the eucharist on Christians' imagination and desire is really quite unfathomable, as though there really is some much-wanted presence there they can be sure of and mustn't miss. Equally remarkable is the way in which the generations have been surprised by the density of meaning in this endlessly repeated rite and ceremonial, even when it is carried through in the most inexpert and tawdry fashion. They have finally come to recognize it as the focus of all that the church knows and wishes to say about him and about life.

As each celebration proceeds it becomes a gathering web of meanings and suggestions, any one of which, at any time, may go further into one's being than the words used or the things done have ever gone, appealing to aspiration we've rarely expressed because of shyness, to griefs and desires normally held in check because we haven't the courage and ability required to articulate them.

And, of course, that's how symbols work. They signify what can't be verbalized. They can sound depths of which we are not consciously aware.

The mind contains more than it collects in one lifetime. Somewhere in its labyrinthine depths is the deposit of centuries, memories of what never happened to us individually but occurred somewhere in the great continuum of evolving life, both human and animal, and left certain vital traces. These hidden depths of thought and feeling in us seem to be reached by the symbolic in the religion and art of the world. Sometimes they are stirred, against all probability, even in the cynical and the despairing. Of all the things Christians do to express and deepen faith it is in the eucharist that, so Wesley thought, one's deep self is most often reached:

> The prayer, the fast, the word conveys,
> When mixed with faith, Thy life to me;
> In all the channels of thy grace
> I still have fellowship with Thee:
> But chiefly here my soul is fed
> With fullness of immortal bread.

Consequently, the eucharist always means much more than it seems to mean, more than our minds can ever take at the time, even when we are in an exceptionally devout phase.

Sometimes we can't take the holy at all, and sometimes we take it eagerly as though we've been thirsty for it for days; but we can never take the full amount of this particular world of love. It's sensible at every eucharist to make an act of faith in that impalpable more that we shall not register just now. It is easy to have the experience and miss the meaning; so it's sensible to affirm the existence of the meaning every so often.

I seem to be going rather a long way round in trying to answer your question, 'What exactly do people receive at the eucharist? As they return from the altar, what do they now have that fine non-sacramentalists like, say, members of the Society of Friends or Salvationists don't have?'

God is not bound by the sacraments of the church. Anyone at all, whatever his religious convictions, or lack of them, at the Father's good pleasure, may have the kingdom. There is nothing better to have anywhere.

And we can't quantify the grace of God. To ask how much, or how much more, of God is here or there is a meaningless exercise. To make comparisons between different Christian traditions, and even different world faiths, as to where there is most of what we're all wanting seems to me to be part of extremely immature religion.

You know as well as I do that there are many traditions in which the desire for God and for understanding why we are here in this confusing world and must shortly leave it are expressed in prayer and conversation and ceremonial. In every one of them that desire gets something of what it desires. No one can use them all. Most people settle for one of them. To do so means necessarily not to have what you have not chosen even to want. You yourself have come to understanding and commitment within sacramental Christianity.

So there does seem to me some, strictly limited, reason for saying that when you go home from Mass you have been given a different experience of Christ from that which the Quaker has in his heart as he goes home from Meeting and that which the Salvationist has been given in the preaching and the singing at the town centre; and clearly you have not been given the blinding light that staggered Saul of Tarsus on the road to Damascus.

What you have been given is what Christians believe God has always given in this way – renewed assurance of his love as revealed in Christ, reminder of your share in the mission and fate of the church, sense of the black pain and cruelty in life, realization of the world's infinite need and infinite redeemability, glimpse of the gathering-up of time, life and death in the praise of God.

All these meanings, and others, can be brought home to us in other ways too by the one God who is all the time responding to human seeking. But the point is that these meanings and assurances are conveyed in this particular way, through this particular rite and ceremonial and the presence known in them, trailing as they do the immeasurable cloud of Christian memory. And that means they have a character all their own and are absolutely unique.

We are not usually reflectively aware of the many deep meanings in the eucharist at the time. We certainly very rarely *feel* the things we believe. It's a help to hold on to no more than one thought. For a simple example, we go up to the altar to re-affirm our view of life. We go up to give ourselves again to God, and to be given to (our offering and his response are two sides of the same coin).

By 'our view of life' I mean that thankfulness and wish to be at one with life and the truth about it that form the way of being human that most appeals to us. We have chosen it because we have seen it in Jesus, the clarity and mercy in which he observed the world, his haunting promises and requests, and the cost to him of his vision of God.

We are consequently much helped by having a place that is just full of him, where what is said and done keep alive for us the Christian faith and recall us to it in the unfortunate casualness of the days when we forget him. The eucharist is that place.

We are often burdened with reminders of the many ways in which we have disappointed our friends and life. We do not believe he had such a burden, though it is said he had another. He didn't drift like us, he was a consecrated man, 'without benefit of clergy', and lived his consecration right through to the bitter end.

So it's not surprising that in the eucharist the church recalls him particularly at that point in his story where his characteristic emotional and spiritual depths are most visible, at the beginning of his last fight when he confronted the choice of avoiding the certain defeat (as far as he could see) of all the passionate hope of his life or going through it into his black tomorrow.

You ask me what you have *got* as, after communicating, you return to your place, hands together, eyes lowered in devotion or confusion. I have a question too. Why this choice of the possessive to cheer one up?

When we return from the altar it is not so much a question of what we have got but what we have just done. We have once again publicly said that we stand with his scruffy crowd that has such a splendid aim – to see life sacramentally, to see all bread and wine, all that's life-sustaining and life-enhancing, as, like the bread and wine of the holy communion, carriers of God's presence, God's meaning, his nourishment and support of us.

It's terrible if you lose your hold on this thought of things and experiences being bearers of spiritual meaning. You then have a much impoverished vocabulary for expressing our reverence before creation, and indeed our fear and distaste before some of it, and our awareness of death whose light step follows close on ours all the time.

We return from the altar having done something, having said our Amen to the great meaning in life he has shown us, and to our place in the vast family of those who have been trying to get this Amen out of their throats for two thousand years.

I'm well aware that they are often nothing to write home about, this multi-national, multi-denominational, never clearly defined rabble that sprawls over the whole world, hating each other's guts in Northern Ireland, obsessed with fear lest women be ordained in England, manning machine-gun positions against Moslems in the Middle East, heroically living and laying down their lives for the poor in South America, for and against the blacks in South Africa, getting the Bible quite wrong here, getting love stupendously right there, quite a few in gaol (a few, perhaps, unjustly), scholars, saints, mystics sprinkled not unnoticeably throughout the whole lot, and every one of them like the rest of humanity wanting some glimpses of earthly happiness before the earth finishes with them. Yet it is under his sign that they are what they are, it is his face they wish to see after this exile. And when we return from the altar we have affirmed that we belong to them, stand with them, engaged in the difficult enterprise of following Jesus, and not disposed to chuck it yet – which means, we think, that he has not taken his Holy Spirit from us.

*   *   *   *   *

The eucharist ended without a blessing. I'm told that this is becoming more customary, the idea being, I suppose, that since the congregation has just communicated they are undoubtedly blessed, as blessed as anyone can be in a darkish world, and to bless them again five minutes later is redundant.

However, I miss the blessing. I don't want purist hands to take it from us.

A blessing does at least two things. It announces God's favour, and it states that what is blessed is to be understood now as having had its significance in the purpose of God affirmed or re-affirmed. So, God is with you. In spite of what you may think when the voice of life seems to spring from little else but pain, you are blessed; what is within you just now, however perplexing, is of that which creates, rescues, inspires, and is certainly leading you further into life's goodness.

There is an immensely profound sense in which these two facts do not need to be stated at the end of the eucharist or at any point during it – because they are always true, and the liturgy itself is one of the ways of proclaiming that. It is always the case that you and I are in God's favour, however wretchedly our story reads. And the very fact that we exist means that we have been created, chosen, set apart in unique individuality, to have our particular unduplicated place in the purpose of God.

The snag is that most of the time we don't believe it. We don't keep such life-giving facts in our heads for long, our minds ruminate many other erroneous and depressing readings of life, and we need these brighter things of Christ called to our remembrance.

There is always, too, the possibility that we may think we are assured of being in God's favour just because we have in fact done our Christian duty and come to the eucharist. That would be an absurd bit of thinking, it would be to see our heavenly Father as altogether just too human, as like so many of us human parents who are pleased with their children when they behave but are apt to withdraw emotionally when they misbehave. God is not like that. He is the eternal love 'above whom is nothing, beyond whom is nothing, without whom is nothing', and he loves us for ourselves, not for our performance.

This truth doesn't always help. Much of the time our minds are not with it; and because it doesn't always help, and blackness is as black as it is, we are never likely to make an assumption of it, much less take it for granted. That, however, doesn't alter the fact that it is the truth and must go on being said, in one way or another and in as many ways as possible; and one of them is as the final sound the eucharist makes in a believer's ears.